101 Western Dressage

Exercises

for Horse & Rider

101 Western Dressage Exercises for Horse & Rider

Jec Aristotle Ballou
and
Stephanie Boyles

Foreword by Al Dunning

Photography by Jason Houston

Storey Publishing

The mission of Storey Publishing is to serve our customers by
publishing practical information that encourages
personal independence in harmony with the environment.

Edited by Deborah Burns and Lisa H. Hiley
Art direction and book design by Cynthia N. McFarland
Layout by Liseann Karandisecky

Photography by © Jason Houston
Arena diagrams by © Stephanie Boyles
Illustrations by Jean Abernethy
Indexed by Susan Olason

Storey books are available at special discounts when purchased in
bulk for premiums and sales promotions as well as for fund-raising or
educational use. Special editions or book excerpts can also be created
to specification. For details, please call 800-827-8673, or send an email
to sales@storey.com.

Storey Publishing
210 MASS MoCA Way
North Adams, MA 01247
www.storey.com

Printed in the United States by Versa Press
10 9 8 7 6 5 4 3 2

LIBRARY OF CONGRESS CATALOGING-IN-PUBLICATION DATA ON FILE

WE GRATEFULLY ACKNOWLEDGE our debt to Frances Carbonnel and her stunning stallions Fino and Estaban, who cheerfully trailered many miles, unloaded in a strange barn, and performed flawlessly under somewhat taxing circumstances to capture these photos.

And we could not have had a lovelier setting or a more gracious host than Angela Seda-Garvin, who opened her facilities to us and on short notice and without blinking an eye pulled Calypso and Rockabye San Doc out of retirement, saddled them up, and then cheerfully agreed to act as a model. Her gorgeous stallion Kiosco SMDR also acted like a star.

Thanks go to David Kaden of Specialized Saddle, who went out of his way to ship us the beautiful Western Dressage–oriented saddle that Fino is wearing on the cover and on page 98.

Finally, we enjoyed working with photographer Jason Houston, who cheerfully met every challenge and figured out how to make it work, while enduring scrutiny and suggestions from almost everyone involved.

Contents

Foreword

IN OVER 40 YEARS OF TRAINING HORSES and riders to their full potential, be it in reining, cutting, showmanship, or any other discipline, I've noticed two things: one, that there's an awful lot of very technical information and equipment out there claiming to improve your horse and your riding; and two, in spite of that, there's still an awful lot of very poor horsemanship in the world. Too many people focus on all that technical stuff and lose sight of the fact that they should be learning for the sake of the horse more than anything else.

Many years ago, when I was training with the great John Hoyt, he told me, "You're doing a fine job riding that horse, but you're so busy thinking about what you're doing that you're not really thinking about what *he's* doing." It took me a while to realize just what he meant by that, but eventually, thinking about what the horse is doing became the foundation of my training methods as well.

It's important to be aware that you can't just sit in the saddle worrying about where to put your legs and what to do with your hands — there's a horse underneath you that needs to be listened to and observed all the time. You have to always be developing your sense of the horse and how he's moving and what he's thinking.

It seems to me that traditional Western riding and classic dressage training have always had more in common than they have differences. The best riders and trainers in both traditions focus on bringing out the best in every horse in a way that works for that horse, rather than imposing a "one way fits all" method. They aren't just making the horse do something, but teaching the horse to want to do that thing and to understand what is expected of it. It's crucial to make a horse's mind as supple and willing as its body.

One of my rules is that you should never be bored riding a horse. You can always make yourself a better rider, which will make your horse better. Sometimes, though, you need to be prodded to see your horse and your riding with fresh eyes, to learn something new and think about things a different way. This book is a terrific tool for helping you do that. There's plenty in here to benefit horses and riders at every level and from every discipline.

Each chapter covers an area of development, such as looseness or adjustability, with good explanations for the importance of each. The exercises can be combined in any way that makes sense for an individual horse or rider. Whether you're looking to refresh or hone your own skills, tune up a performance horse, or start a youngster from scratch, you'll find *101 Western Dressage Exercises* useful, informative, and worthwhile.

–AL DUNNING
Scottsdale, Arizona

CHAPTER 1

WHAT IS WESTERN DRESSAGE?

AT ITS CORE, Western Dressage is no different from classical dressage. Many Western horsemen agree that the goals and methods for training a Western horse are the same as those used over centuries among classical dressage enthusiasts. The relatively new discipline of Western Dressage bridges the alleged separation that has existed between these two worlds, bringing together the history and culture of horsemanship of the American West and the ancient traditions of dressage practiced in institutions such as the Spanish Riding School.

Some say it combines the superb, almost intuitive riding of American cowboys with the systematic training methods of venerable European institutions. Western Dressage also acknowledges and embraces the fact that the typical Western stock horse is built differently from the breeds most often seen in today's classical dressage ring.

For many, this marriage was only a matter of time. With its commitment to harmony, lightness, good horse-human connection and communication, and athleticism, Western riding is a natural development for dressage. Western Dressage uses the principles of classical dressage to improve the balance, cadence, and carriage of a horse.

Following a progressive training path similar to that of traditional dressage, Western Dressage begins with an individual horse's natural ability to carry himself and uses increasingly more difficult gymnastic exercises to improve that ability. Some of the ongoing goals include a horse that moves with his center of gravity shifted toward the rear; has greater elasticity in his muscles; shows responsiveness to the aids; and demonstrates perfection of longitudinal and lateral

balance. Overall, the horse should be able to work with ease and grace through progressively difficult patterns and exercises.

Competitive dressage horse

Western Pleasure horse

What Does Western Dressage Look Like?

A Western Dressage horse moving correctly on the bit should demonstrate that he stretches into the rider's contact. He should not be shown with a draped rein. Instead, there should be *light* rein tone evident between horse and rider. It should appear that the horse is seeking a feel of the rider's hands, with his neck arching and stretching forward from his body. You might say that he "looks through" the bridle. Using strong, visible rein cues, constantly bumping the bit, or causing a horse to gape his mouth are considered serious faults. Special emphasis is given to a quiet mouth with head carriage that reflects the appropriate degree of collection and balance for each individual horse.

Head and neck carriage are the result of the Western Dressage horse's learning to carry the rest of his body in balance. Riders must not take shortcuts to create a headset prior to the horse's learning to use his body properly. Riding either one- or two-handed is permitted, as is using a snaffle or curb bit. Riders choose the best option for themselves and their mounts.

The gaits for Western Dressage — walk, jog, and lope — parallel those of traditional dressage, allowing for the fact that Western Dressage is suited to a different conformation and type of horse, generally speaking. The discipline grew out of a sequential and fine-tuned method of improving and showing off the movement and athletic feats of a stock horse. The responsiveness, suppleness, and maneuverability of a well-trained stock horse translate readily into a style of dressage that focuses on softness and willingness.

Western Dressage horse

No one expects a 17-hand warmblood to excel at cutting and barrel racing, and in Western Dressage, no one expects the suspension and animation of gaits that is so sought after in the current dressage show circuit.

The Western Dressage horse should move with impulsion, a forward-thinking attitude, engagement, and looseness. He should be highly maneuverable and his stride quickly adjustable. His gaits should demonstrate a good swinging stride length respective to his type, but his stride length in walk, jog, and lope is not expected to be either as extravagant or as ground-covering as the gaits commonly demanded in today's competitive dressage arenas.

A clear difference is drawn between the movement seen in modern Western Pleasure–type competitions and the movement expected in Western Dressage. The latter discipline expects a more forward-moving horse. While emphasis is not placed on a high level of suspension in the gaits, a very slow-moving and dull gait is not rewarded.

Western Dressage Movement

The general assumption is that a Western horse moves slowly. But this is not necessarily the case either in a ground-covering stock horse or in Western Dressage. That the Western Dressage horse moves well is more important than how rapidly or slowly he jogs or lopes. Like practicing yoga, in training the Western Dressage horse, any slowness of gaits must come as a result of correct gymnastic development: a swinging back, pushing and flexed hindquarters, longitudinal balance in all three gaits, acceptance of the contact, symmetry, and straightness.

Slow-moving gaits are not an end goal unto themselves; they should be proof of balance, the result of correct training that includes schooling in lively, working gaits. The correct tempo for each Western Dressage horse differs according to his individual conformation, limb length, and ability to flex his hindquarters. As the horse's balance and strength increase and he is able therefore to carry more weight on his hindquarters, his tempo will naturally slow down. What he gains in loftiness and joint flexion and a softly swinging back, he trades for the quicker "falling on the forehand" gaits of an undeveloped, unbalanced horse. This is the progression we aim to see in Western Dressage.

Asking the horse to travel slowly before his musculature and balance are prepared creates compromises in joint flexion and flaws in movement. When riders try to satisfy a "look" or trend of slow-moving Western gaits without first training the horse to move with a rounded and swinging back and actively flexed hind joints, the horse blocks his back, essentially freezing the bridge between his hindquarters and forehand. The muscles along his spine and upper neck become rigid, his chest tightens, and the hind legs eventually become stiff from lack of hip and stifle flexion.

WESTERN DRESSAGE COMPETITION

For competitions, working Western attire and equipment are the norm, rather than the flashier show-ring styles seen in most Western competition, although some silver trim and a sparkly shirt can be appreciated. Helmets in the show ring are optional at this point, although as riders and trainers, we strongly endorse helmet use at all times.

For everyday schooling, riders are encouraged to ride in whatever equipment and gear allows them to achieve their goals. Many modern stock-type or all-purpose saddles are suitable. A close-contact saddle with stirrups set to allow the rider's heel to fall under the hip is generally best for enabling the rider to communicate closely and clearly with subtle leg cues. Saddles with bulky fenders or large rigging systems for the cinch will pose challenges for riders.

Western Dressage was officially branded in the United States in 2010, and in 2013 the United States Equestrian Federation named the Western Dressage Association of America an affiliate organization with its own chapter in the USEF rule book. For up-to-date rules about equipment and tests, visit www.westerndressageassociation.org. See a sample test on page 21.

Before You Begin

The exercises in this book are most successful when they follow a suitable period of warming up. But what makes a warm-up good? Is an active one better than a slow, relaxing one? How long — or short — should it be? Many riders with good intentions believe that spending some time moving their horses around either on the longe line or under saddle prior to their workout counts as adequate preparation. Unfortunately, this isn't the case. In fact, a proper warm-up governs the success of your training session.

From a physiological standpoint, the warm-up determines how much conditioning and positive physical response your horse will — or won't — receive from your training. This means that since we dressage riders aim to make our horses stronger, fitter, and more supple every day, our preworkout routine can either help or hinder us.

First, let's clarify the distinction between loosening up and warming up. These are two different activities; you need to do both before your workout. Loosening up lubricates the joints and starts the flow of fluids and electrolytes between soft tissues. The goal of warming up is to increase oxygen delivery and blood circulation to the horse's skeletal muscles to prevent early accumulation of metabolic wastes such as lactic acid in the tissues.

In addition to causing early fatigue, lactic acid buildup also prohibits the horse from benefiting from the workout because it changes the muscles' pH levels, which controls their ability to contract and relax. To counter this, and to receive the benefit of exercising the muscles, you want to stimulate enough oxygen and blood flow to the horse's muscles to optimize them for performance.

Loosening Up

Whenever you first mount up or begin longeing, you should spend 3 to 5 minutes allowing your horse to walk around in a relaxed posture without any restrictive rein contact. Some choose to do this portion in-hand, while others like to hack around their properties. This gentle activity allows the horse's joint fluids to become less viscous and lubricate the sockets. Studies have shown that it can take several minutes of slow movement for joint fluids to circulate fully for horses that live in mostly confined accommodations.

It is important that a horse's muscles not be in a contracted state, such as when a horse is ridden in a collected frame or longed with side reins. Joints must be allowed to move through their full range of motion prior to being held in a static position during dressage exercise with a rounded frame. At the beginning of a riding session, the oxygen, blood flow, and fuel necessary to support the contraction-relaxation cycle of functioning muscle fibers aren't present; asking muscles to engage immediately when the horse comes from his stall before these elements circulate essentially chokes them off.

In a resting state, only 15 percent of circulating blood is delivered to the horse's muscles, with the remainder traveling instead to his organs and digestive system. During exercise, however, up to 85 percent of his blood circulates to his muscles. One of the goals of loosening up is to allow this shift to happen.

Warming Up

Once you have things loosened up a bit, it is time to begin the more strenuous activity of warming up. Here you want to begin asking the horse to stretch into contact but not be in a collected frame. Avoid

Lateral movements rank among the most valuable tools you can use with the horse. When correctly performed, they combine a suppling and strengthening effect. This cannot be said, however, when lateral exercises are ridden too soon in a horse's training or with tempos that are rushed or imbalanced. Many riders are in a hurry to begin lateral movements with their horses before longitudinal balance is secured. This is a grave mistake. The consistency and rhythm of the horse's working gaits must be confirmed prior to schooling lateral movements.

When the horse's hind legs step sideways under his body, they create a stretching effect that runs throughout the musculature of his hindquarters. His long back muscles and the obliques that connect through fascia with these hindquarter muscles are also stretched. Developing suppleness in these areas creates harmonious and expressive movement.

Lateral movements also stretch the outside of the body while contracting the inside. Practiced equally in both directions, they lead a horse to better skeletal straightness and symmetry. Improved straightness is a constant goal, and exercises such as shoulder-in, haunches-in, and the variety of leg-yielding patterns available bring us ever closer.

The strengthening effect follows from how the horse must organize his body during these maneuvers. First, he brings his hind legs closer together, which loads the inside leg with more weight. When suppleness is present, this added load increases the flexion of hind joints. Think of the similarity here with humans performing squats with a narrow base. Meanwhile his obliques and abdominal musculature become toned in order to keep his trunk balanced in this position.

If horses are not prepared adequately for lateral movements, they will become more stiff and crooked rather than less so. These horses will lose balance or stiffen against the exercise, which locks the stifle joint, which in turn blocks movement from coming through the horse's back. In this scenario, the horse is training himself to move with restriction and tension. Rather than flexing through his body and properly tensioning the trunk muscles to draw his hind legs under the body, he will compromise his posture to get himself through the exercise, but he does so with choppy gaits and no improvement of his body.

This is similar to humans tackling exercises beyond the athletic reach of their bodies. They might clench their teeth and grunt through 20 push-ups, for example, but they do so with poor form and therefore create only rigidity. The muscles they aim to strengthen are either overly tensioned or avoided, neither of which creates improvement. Western Dressage training and competitions follow a systematic progression for gradually introducing lateral movements as the rest of the horse's performance evolves. This progression is necessary for correct development.

the common mistake of performing suppling exercises at the start of this warm-up phase before sufficient oxygen and blood flow in the tissues and their subsequent rise in temperature give them pliability. Cold and unfueled muscle fibers, tendons, and ligaments are susceptible to overstretching injuries. Also, if there is tension in an antagonistic muscle group, suppling movements will cause inefficient use of the horse's body and contribute to side dominance.

It is best, physiologically, to spend the first 5 minutes of this phase with active forward movement in either jog or lope. Which gait you choose depends on each individual horse. Some are more balanced in the jog, others prefer to lope. The key here is to maintain an active gait with the goal of stimulating the skeletal muscles enough to force blood flow to them. This does not happen at a leisurely pace.

After 5 to 10 minutes of active movement, the skeletal muscles are warm enough to begin suppling exercises. These can include various-size circles, leg-yielding, and bends such as loopy serpentines. As this phase of warming up continues, *progressively* increase the intensity of muscle output and suppling by using smaller circles and more difficult lateral movements.

As you proceed from this stage, your warm-up exercises should lead you directly into your planned workout for the day. This is to say that your warm-up should flow seamlessly into your schooling session; you should not take a break in between. At this point, the horse's muscles are able to contract more powerfully, which enhances the quality of his performance and ensures a better training session. All exercises performed will now have a greater strengthening and suppling benefit.

What to Look For

Every horse should feel — and look — different after a proper warm-up period. It's like shaking out the cobwebs from the corners. Learn to observe and feel your horse's movement at the 2-minute point in your warm-up, then the 5-minute, and at the end. What changes can you detect? Look for looseness, longer strides, more responsiveness to your aids, and physical signs that he is ready for work (e.g., warm muscles, salivating mouth, freely swinging tail, mental focus).

Do not assume that if your horse has access to a turnout paddock, he is already warmed up for you to ride. Horses in their natural state spend a lot of their time standing still, punctuated with short bursts of energy. This kind of movement does not prepare their muscles and joint fluid, blood, and electrolyte circulation for the kind of *consistent* movement and energy expenditure we require in dressage. Also remember that we need to warm up the horse specifically for the kind of movements we'll be performing, so that means he needs to be warmed up stretching through to the contact in order to exercise his back, topline, and haunches. Even if he has been in turnout, he will not do this on his own!

Introduction to the Exercises

This book was written for you — the eager rider, the accomplished trainer, the horse lover, the student. Don't let it settle into a spot on your bookshelf or your coffee table. It should end up dirty, dog-eared, creased, and bookmarked from being dragged out at all your training sessions. Its purpose is to inspire you with ideas, provide specific skills to practice, and motivate you to keep improving. When you want follow-up material from the last lesson with your trainer, look no further. When you need some help improving your horse's performance, flip open the cover and take your pick of exercises.

These exercises took form through years of training horses and studying equine exercise physiology. They are some of the best for improving a horse's athletic performance with specific regard to collection, balance, and suppleness. They are all excellent schooling opportunities, but, as with all interactions with your horse, listen to the moment and be willing to adapt to the moment. Feel free to amend any exercise as needed if your horse acts overwhelmed, frustrated, or fatigued.

This book is not intended to be read from start to finish or front to back. Its layout enables you to delve in wherever you choose on any given day. Exercises are rated in terms of difficulty. Beginner exercises are suitable for inexperienced riders, young horses, new dressage students, or timid riders. Intermediate exercises are geared toward medium-level riders whose horses possess adequate fitness. Advanced exercises are the most difficult, requiring collection, command of lateral movements, and higher-level maneuvering. Find the exercises that challenge and please you but are not a total struggle.

WHY ALL THE POLES?

If you are wondering why so many of these dressage exercises use ground poles, there is no shortage of good reasons. Consistent work over ground poles in rhythmic gaits with a rounded topline leads to all kinds of positive results. Primarily, it helps create stifle flexion in the hind legs, which sets off a chain reaction of other desirable effects. Because of the interconnectedness of the horse's hindquarter musculature through fascia, this controlled stifle flexion also positively taxes abdominal muscles, draws the hind legs further under the body, and supples the low back. Using ground poles is a way to work smarter, not harder. Allow the pole patterns to activate your horse's hind legs, and you can then be quieter as the rider without using busy or strong aids.

By virtue of their fixed spacing, poles develop cadence and balance in the horse's gaits by controlling foot placement, which confirms regularity in the stride rhythm. The horse achieves animation in his limbs and precision of limb movement. The oscillating effect on spinal vertebrae and rounded flexion accomplished by balanced travel over poles helps eliminate stiffness in the neck and hindquarters. By creating a horse that is looser in the topline and more attentive about stride and foot placement, you are making a stronger horse.

The late Dr. Reiner Klimke, multiple Olympic gold medalist and German riding master, credited the weekly use of ground pole exercises for his historic dressage success. In addition to their unrivaled conditioning results, these types of exercises made a more effective rider, in his view. Many top dressage riders to this day use some form of work with poles on a regular basis, from simple patterns on straight lines to raised cavalletti to gymnastic jumping.

The value of this kind of training cannot be overstated, although it bears mentioning that benefits are unaccomplished if practice happens less than one to two times every week. Otherwise you will not see gains, due to lack of recruiting the horse's musculature often enough. Physiological adaptation only happens with frequent practice.

These exercises are not expected to stand alone as complete workouts. They are most useful when blended into a warm-up and cool-down routine in addition to other work you may have planned for your day. You are the artist. These exercises give you a complete palette from which to choose and mix as you see fit. Enjoy the journey!

You will derive the most from these exercises by choosing two or three each week that are comfortably within your current level of training, plus two that are a bit of a stretch for either you or your horse.

For instance, if your horse is reasonably fit and has been in regular training for a year or more and has just begun working on developing more hindquarter engagement, you might focus on three easier exercises from the Softness chapter throughout the week in addition to two exercises from the Engagement chapter that he may struggle with slightly. This way you will be confirming basics and improving relaxation and confidence while also making progress.

As with any athlete, it is important not to work at the same intensity level every day. This kind of repetitiveness leads to physical and mental burnout. It also creates a sluggish nervous system with muscles that only recruit at a single rate of speed and force. For mental freshness and physical benefits, it is far more productive to alternate the difficulty of your sessions.

DRESSAGE MOVEMENTS: A VISUAL GLOSSARY

Here is a visual guide to the dressage movements you will use in this book. Underneath each drawing is an icon that represents that movement in the arena diagrams that accompany the exercises.

collected walk	collected jog	collected lope
· ·	– – – – – – – – –	o · o · o · o · o · o ·

working walk	working jog	working lope
· · · · · · · · · · · · ·	– – – – – – – –	– – o – – o – – o – – o

free walk	lengthened jog	counter-lope
· · · · · · · · ·	— — — — —	– – o – – o – – o – – o

lengthened walk	stretching jog	lengthened lope
· · · · · · ·	— — — — —	– – o – – o – – o

start ⭐

halt ✳

rein back ↔ ↔

transition —

flying change ‖

ground pole ▬▬

raised ground pole ✕▬▬✕

cross rail ◁▷

cone ▲

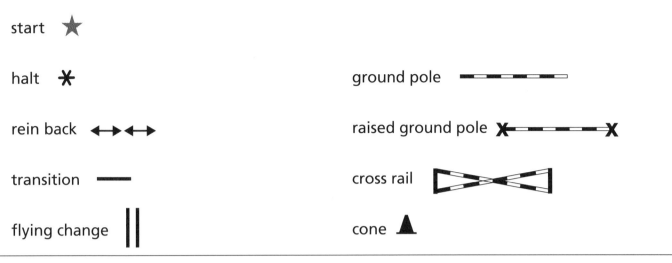

turn on forehand   turn on haunches

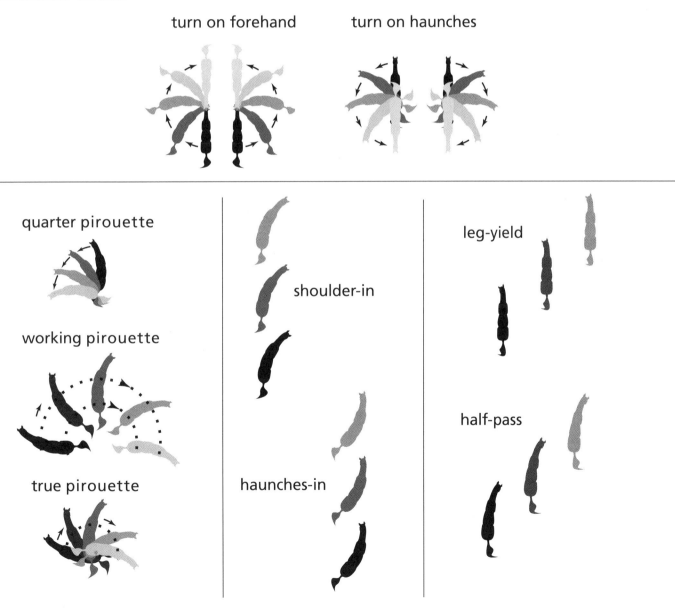

quarter pirouette

working pirouette

true pirouette

shoulder-in

haunches-in

leg-yield

half-pass

MONDAY

45- to 60-minute Loosening Session

Work on suppling your horse's whole body, both longitudinally and laterally. Ride your horse in a long and low frame in all three gaits, stretching his topline forward and downward. Practice lots of bending figures. Ride basic lateral movements such as leg-yielding and turns on forehand and haunches but also ones requiring more engagement, such as half-pass and pirouettes. Ride numerous gait transitions between all the gaits, ensuring they are smooth and graceful. Be sure to include a sustained period of loping, including a variety of figures.

TUESDAY

Introduce New Material

Following a 20-minute warm-up, introduce a new exercise from this book to confirm or introduce a movement that is not yet confirmed for your horse, such as tighter bends, counter-lope, or lateral movements. Finish the session with exercises that your horse knows and does well already.

WEDNESDAY

Ground Work or Trail Ride

Take a break from riding in the arena and allow your horse to use his body differently. This prevents repetitive motion injuries and also wards off mental burnout. It also prevents the horse's back muscles from becoming rigid or blocked.

THURSDAY

Building

Either build on Tuesday's work or introduce a new exercise from this book that is a slight stretch but within reach of your horse's current level of training.

FRIDAY

Fitness

Spend an hour working on cardiovascular fitness: ride up and down hills, lope for prolonged periods of time, take an active 1-hour trail ride that includes lots of jogging, or cross-train with small jumps, either in the arena or cross-country.

SATURDAY

Confirmed Movements

Use this day to tour through your development level. After warming up, ride your horse at his current performance level, executing every movement and transition that he has confirmed to date. This will include various figures in working or collected gaits, lateral movements, lope patterns, and so on.

Keep your standards as high as though you were riding at a competition. You may even choose to ride through a dressage test at your current level.

SUNDAY

OFF

Western Dressage Association of America

2013 Western Dressage Test ~ Level 2, Test 3

Purpose: To confirm that the horse has developed impulsion; accepts more weight on the hindquarters; moves with an uphill tendency especially at collected paces; and is reliable and light on the bit. Demonstrate a greater degree of collection, engagement, lateral balance, straightness, bending, suppleness, and self-carriage. Rideability is emphasized.

1	A X	Enter collected jog Halt, salute Proceed collected jog	Straightness; quality of the jog; balance in downward transition; square, straight halt; immobility; willingness when asked
2	C	Track right, collected jog	Balance and correct bend in turn; quality of the jog
3	M-X-K	Lengthen the stride in the jog	Balance; straightness; length of stride; maintenance of tempo
4	K	Collected jog	Balance of transition; quality of the jog
5	B	Track left, collect jog	Balance and correct bend in turn; quality of the jog
6	X	Halt 5 seconds	Balance in downward transition; square, straight halt; immobility; willingness when asked
7	X	360-degree turn on haunches left	Pivot, step, pivot, step, turn on inside hind leg; maintenance of the rhythm; correct flexion to the left
8	X	Collected lope, left lead, circle left 10 meters	Balance in transition; roundness, balance and correct bend on circle; quality of the lope
9	X	Circle left 20 meters, lengthening lope	Roundness, balance and correct bend on circle; length of stride; maintenance of tempo; quality of the lope
10	X	Collected lope, proceed straight ahead	Balance in transition; quality of the lope
11	E	Track left, collected lope	Balance and correct bend in turn; quality of the lope
12	A - C	Serpentine 3 equal loops, quarter line to quarter line, maintain the left lead	Balance, bend and correct placement of the loops; quality of the lope
13	C	Working walk	Balance in transition; quality of the walk
14	H-X-F	Free walk	Walk with horse willing and able to stretch the neck down and forward; relaxation; rhythm; swing through the back
15	F	Working walk	Balance in transition; quality of the walk
16	A	Working jog	Balance in transition; quality of the jog
17	E	Track right, working jog	Balance and correct bend in turn; quality of the jog
18	X	Halt 5 seconds	Balance in downward transition; square, straight halt; immobility; willingness when asked
19	X	360-degree turn on haunches right	Pivot, step, pivot, step, turn on inside hind leg; maintenance of the rhythm; correct flexion to the right
20	X	Collected lope, right lead, circle right 10 meters	Balance in transition; roundness, balance and correct bend on circle; quality of the lope
21	X	Circle right 20 meters, lengthening lope	Roundness, balance and correct bend on circle; length of stride; maintenance of tempo; quality of the lope
22	X	Collected lope, proceed straight ahead	Balance in transition; quality of the lope
23	B	Track right, collected lope	Balance and correct bend in turn; quality of the lope
24	A - C	Serpentine 3 equal loops, quarter line to quarter line, maintain the right lead	Balance, bend and correct placement of the loops; quality of the lope
25	C	Collected jog	Balance in transition; quality of the jog
26	M-X-K	Lengthen the stride in the jog	Balance; straightness; length of stride; maintenance of tempo
27	K	Collect jog	Balance in transition; quality of the jog
28	A	Turn left down the centerline	Balance and correct bend in turn; quality of the jog
29	X	Halt, salute	Balance in downward transition; square, straight halt; immobility

Leave arena at A in a walk with long or looped reins.

Adapted with permisison from WDAA

CHAPTER 2
SOFTNESS

"SOFTNESS" IS ONE OF THOSE ELUSIVE TERMS tossed around in clinics and training situations and, while difficult to define precisely, this concept is at the heart of Western Dressage. Simply stated, softness is the prompt, willing, and effortless responsiveness of a horse to his rider's cues. In dressage texts, this concept is commonly used synonymously with lightness. For centuries, classical dressage manuals have encouraged people to ride their horses in a state of lightness, rather than coercing them around the arena with strong aids and overly active reins.

Riding a horse that is "soft" feels easy. He moves quickly with minimal pressure from your cues, he carries himself lightly in the reins, and his gaits are comfortable to ride. Contrast this with a horse who feels stiff in his body when you use your legs, or one that responds rigidly to one or both reins. Western Dressage strongly emphasizes softness because it illustrates correct, thorough, and progressive training. It also underscores the relationship between horse and rider.

Try It Yourself

For many riders, however, softness might be something they have not yet felt if they haven't had the luxury of riding horses other than their own. Their task is to learn and feel how wonderfully responsive a horse can be under them. The simplest way to do this is to take inventory of your own horse's responses. Try this: from a standstill, ask your horse to walk off with the lightest leg cue imaginable (think of a fly landing on the horse's side). Count the seconds until he responds. If you find yourself counting "One, two . . ." your horse is not as responsive as he needs to be. He should step off instantly.

Likewise, ask your horse with a light touch from your leg to move from a standstill one step sideways to the left. Does he do it immediately, without throwing his head up, bracing his neck, or resisting your leg? These are indications of how soft your horse is and where you might need to do more work.

Take Your Time

If you find that negotiating some of these patterns requires a lot of effort on your part, your horse needs more softness. It is worth noting that, obviously, only a horse that is comfortable in his body will be soft to ride. A sore horse or one wearing an ill-fitting saddle first needs to have such issues remedied. Also, retraining a horse out of long-standing postural habits requires time and body therapies before he is able to achieve true softness under saddle. A rider cannot expect to achieve immediate softness with a horse that has spent years bracing his jaw or neck, for instance. This kind of rehab must include massage and unmounted bodywork to undo old habits.

By working through the exercises presented here, you should notice your horse becoming more responsive to lighter cues. He should also begin to feel like his body is more pliable and less resistant to accomplishing these tasks. These are prime characteristics to make note of every day. Some days, he will be softer than others, and it will be helpful to keep track.

1. Correct Flexion

LEVEL: **BEGINNER**

One of the quickest and most critical ways to develop better movement and rideability in your horse is to improve looseness in his poll and neck. Think of his poll as a control center for his body's mechanics. Many riders do not realize how much this region governs the horse's way of going, but the attitude of the neck determines the attitude of the body. Therefore, a tight or restricted poll produces the same kind of body. A nicely supple poll that flexes smoothly from side to side, as well as up and down, allows loose movement throughout the horse's body.

Lateral poll flexions are beneficial for most horses before riding, especially those that tend to be one-sided. By encouraging mobility and adequate spacing in the first vertebral joint, these flexions prevent or resolve restrictions in the horse's neck that occur from tension buildup, bit pressure on the jaw, and other performance strains.

Helpful Hints

★ Keep your hand well in front of the saddle when asking for flexion.

★ Keep your hand close to your horse's neck.

★ Do not raise the rein over or across your horse's withers.

★ Keep a feel on the outside rein so that your horse has something to flex into.

1 Begin in a square, balanced halt with your horse on the bit and stretching into the reins. Hold the reins with both hands.

2 With your right hand, flex your wrist inward to bring your knuckles closer toward your horse's neck.

3 Ask your horse to flex his head to the right. You do not want him to turn his neck, just swivel his head.

4 Once he flexes his head to the right and you can see his eye, allow him to straighten back out so that you resume even tension on both reins.

5 Repeat the bend to the left side. Repeat the sequence three times on each side.

2. Releasing Tension

LEVEL: **BEGINNER**

The roots of crookedness are numerous, but the general cause begins — and worsens — when a horse becomes uneven in his musculature. One side develops tighter, shorter muscles while the other side is more permanently stretched open. For Western Dressage movements to be graceful and fully correct, riders need to remedy this natural crookedness, prioritizing it above the later training results of impulsion, collection, and extension, which cannot happen without straightness.

Exercises that alternately stretch and flex each side of the horse's body are most effective because they prohibit the horse from traveling in his habitual posture that favors one direction over the other. Frequent direction changes prevent the horse from getting blocked against the rider's aids on his more difficult side and help him use his hind legs equally by repeatedly changing which leg is on the inside. This encourages a good pattern of flexing and then stretching each side of the horse, leading to better symmetry.

This exercise also encourages looseness and stretchiness in the horse's topline, helping his spinal vertebrae oscillate and swing freely. This kind of unrestricted motion in the horse's back is critical for achieving straightness and balance. After several repetitions of this pattern, your horse should feel very adjustable and supple.

Helpful Hint

★ Time yourself. Strive to maintain a brisk lope for at least 60 seconds in each direction before transitioning downward.

1 Shorten your stirrups one or two holes from their normal length.

2 Lift your seat so that you are hovering 4 to 6 inches out of the saddle.

3 Stretch down into your deeply flexed ankles and torso, bending slightly forward from the waist. Visualize yourself in a squatting position like a downhill ski racer, with bent knees and slightly angled upper body.

4 Pick up the lope on a large oval. Allow the horse to stretch his neck out with his nose clearly ahead of vertical.

5 Encourage him to really move out while you remain in your light seat off his back.

6 Once he starts to release and move with energy, modify your oval. Continue galloping but use your outside leg to "squeeze" in the sides of your oval a few meters on each side to make a fat hourglass figure.

7 Repeat the pattern in both directions.

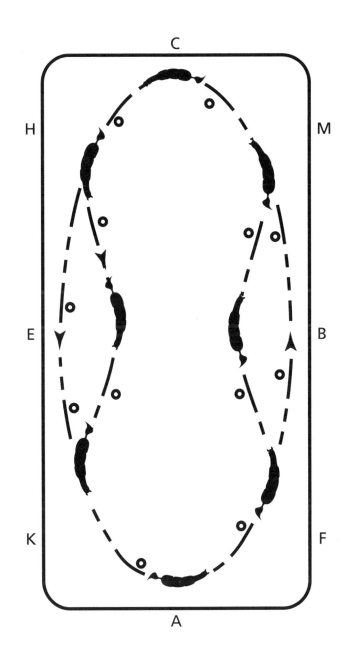

KEY

lope

3. Arena Diamond

LEVEL: BEGINNER

All good trainers know that if you ask a horse to perform exercises that manipulate his body the right way, results will fall into your lap, often rapidly. Because of how interconnected the horse's muscular and skeletal systems are, relatively simple yet strategic maneuvers can have far-reaching effects. If you have ever strung together a few key yoga maneuvers, you have likely experienced this effect on your own body. Your posture, balance, and strength were immediately improved by your actions.

This pattern asks the horse to make frequent adjustments of stride, which recruit different muscle fibers at varying rates of effort and alleviate any tendency to become blocked against the rider, dull to the aids, or listless. Consistently reorganizing his body creates energy in the hind legs and lightness in the forehand while preventing the flat, heavy movement that arises from repetitive motion.

Helpful Hints

★ Turn your horse from your seat, not the reins, at each diamond point. Think of steering his withers rather than his head and neck. Close your inside bending leg against his rib cage while positioning your outside leg slightly back, using it with light thigh pressure to turn the withers to the next focal point.

★ Ride as if you intend to ride straight through the fence at each letter. Do not start turning before you get there; otherwise your horse will drift out through his outside shoulder.

★ Keep your rein contact absolutely equal throughout the pattern. Don't throw it away on the straight lines.

1 Develop a working jog, tracking right.

2 At **A**, turn off the rail directly toward **E**. (You will be riding a mini diagonal line; do *not* ride into the corner between **A** and **K**.)

3 Arrive at the rail at **E** and proceed only one stride.

4 Then turn and ride toward **C**.

5 Continue following the diamond pattern as shown in the diagram.

6 Once you are riding the figure accurately, at each point of the diamond slow down to a slow jog as you round the turn and then immediately lengthen the strides between each point.

7 Once this is going smoothly, lope the figure with the same variation in stride.

8 Repeat in the other direction.

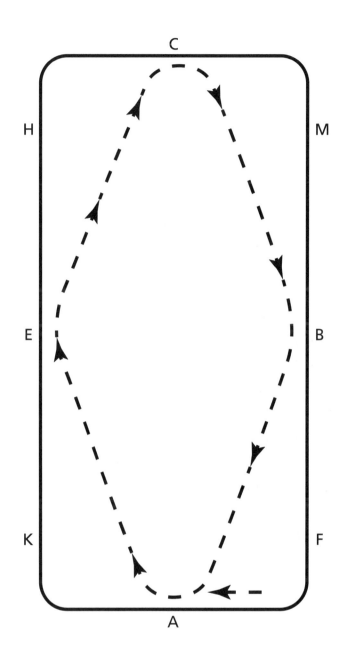

K E Y

working jog

- - - - - - - - -

4. Random Rails

LEVEL: **BEGINNER**

Like us, horses move their bodies and limbs by utilizing a well-worn circuitry of nerves that signal muscles to fire. In order to create *different* movement — a more uphill lope, for example, or a smoother jog — we need to alter this ingrained pattern by developing new circuitry in his nervous system and musculature that will allow that movement to evolve. Once you have motor neurons firing in a new way, you open the door to reinventing your horse's way of going.

This exercise works by shaking the horse out of his rut. It mixes up his usual patterns of footfalls and interrupts his muscle memory. It works especially well with horses that travel heavily on the forehand or tend to get crooked and lean on one shoulder. It keeps these horses using their bodies more fully than just slogging around the arena using the same speed, length, and animation of stride as usual.

Helpful Hints

★ Always prepare for your chosen line well ahead.

★ Make no abrupt turns.

★ Ask yourself if you are making it clear to your horse what you expect and where he is to head. Be sure he stays with you and does not start making up his own plan.

1 Place ground poles at various places around the arena in no particular order. The diagram is a suggestion only. Be creative!

2 Come up with a variety of patterns to approach the poles using both arcs and straight lines.

3 After riding through a few different patterns in one pace, ride over the poles in different paces within the jog (e.g., collected jog, working jog, lengthened jog).

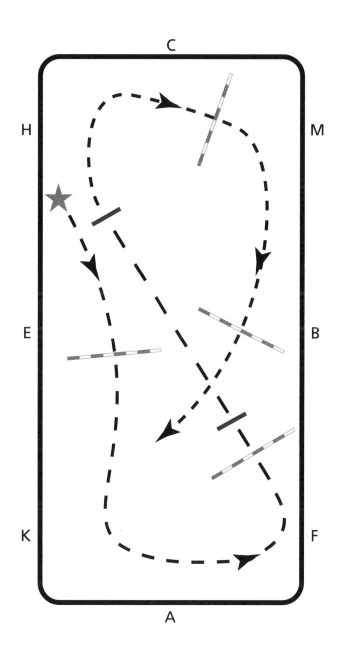

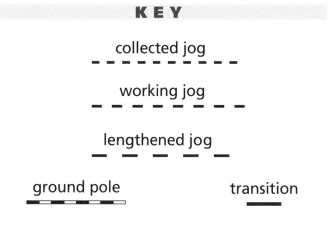

KEY

collected jog

working jog

lengthened jog

ground pole   transition

5. Serpentine with Poles

LEVEL: **BEGINNER**

BENEFITS

Whether we want more bend or impulsion or roundness, we should remember that well-ridden figures are our sharpest tools. Well ridden in this case means accurate and rhythmic. More often than not, riders end up with vaguely defined figures: wobbly circles, wandering turns, and so on. The downside of this, aside from being unclear to the horse, is that the rider loses communication with the horse's hind legs and the horse develops poor alignment, usually becoming crooked in the direction of his dominant side.

The solution is to practice figures that force the rider to pay attention. This exercise is an excellent tool to coordinate a rider's aids. It requires making subtle but clear shifts in geometry that bring more control and engagement to the horse's hind legs. When this happens, other delightful things start happening, such as collection, self-carriage, and lightness.

Helpful Hints

★ Maintain symmetry on the loops of your serpentine.

★ Each arc needs to be the same size and shape for this figure to flow smoothly.

1 Set poles two jog strides apart (approximately 8 feet).

2 Begin in a working jog before **A**. Turn toward the poles and ride straight over them.

3 Turn left and ride between the last two poles.

4 Serpentine your way through the remaining poles.

5 At the end, turn and ride over the poles again.

6 Serpentine back through them.

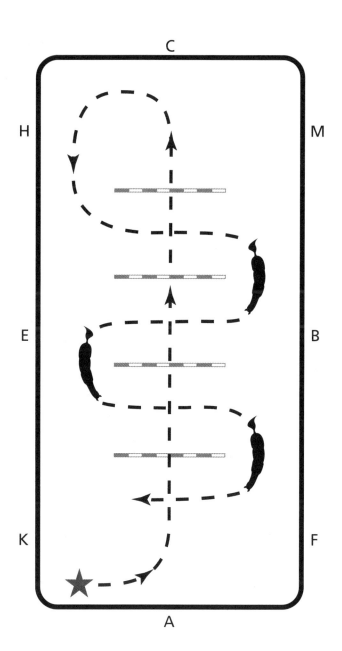

KEY

working jog

ground pole

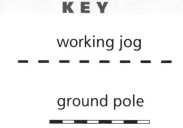

6. Haunches-in Prep

LEVEL: **BEGINNER**

BENEFITS

Prior to beginning any movements that require a haunches-in position, it is beneficial to first achieve a level of training that demonstrates consistent rhythm, balance, and bend on 10-meter circles, shoulder-in, and leg-yields. Confirming this foundation will ensure that your horse can hold his body in a laterally flexed position without falling apart and recruiting — or stiffening — muscles and joints we are not targeting. This will also ensure that your horse is adequately conditioned, as haunches-in maneuvers, like counter-lope, place a fair bit of torque on the horse's lower back and outside hip stabilizers.

Once you are ready to begin haunches-in, intro-duce positioning and footwork with this routine, which relies on an arena rail to give both you and your horse the correct alignment from the very first step. When riders can learn to do haunches-in cor-rectly right from the start, it saves them a lot of frus-tration down the road.

One of the biggest pitfalls for riders is simply pushing the horse's hindquarters over without main-taining the correct bend through his whole body. Remember that this bent position around your inner leg is just as important as how far you can move his haunches over.

Helpful Hints

★ Be sure to keep your horse's neck parallel to the fence rail, so that his chest and shoulders point straight down the track. They are not angled toward the rail.

★ Your horse should have slight inside flexion at his poll but should not be overbent with his forehead facing into the arena.

★ Patient work on this exercise teaches your horse the correct angle and bend for haunches-in. With repetition, you will eliminate the guessing and cheating that often accompanies this movement.

1 Ask your horse to stand in a quiet halt along the rail while remaining on the bit.

2 Close your inside (right) leg against his side for support. Ask with your inside rein for him to turn his head to the right.

3 Without allowing his front feet to move, ask him to step his haunches away from the rail by positioning your outside leg 2 inches back and pressing lightly. Remain weighted on your inside seat bone as you do this.

4 Bring his haunches in only enough to line up his left hip and right shoulder.

5 Ask him to stand quietly in this alignment.

6 Repeat in the opposite direction.

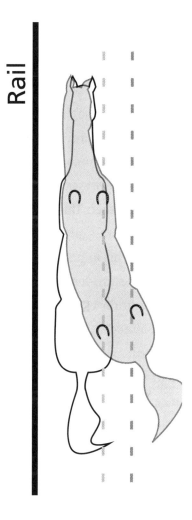

Rail

7. Circle 8s

BENEFITS

In a perfect ride, the horse should travel with a loose spine correctly centered, a supple neck, and equal weight in each of the four corners of his body so that he feels solid underneath you rather than leaking out one side or the other. This alignment — or straightness, to use dressage jargon — ensures that the horse is flexing his joints correctly. Riding with crookedness creates uneven torque and strain, which results in sore or undeveloped muscles.

Most riders already know that performing arena figures at different gaits is on par with guiding your horse through yoga poses. It leads the way to alignment, balance, and hindquarter engagement. Keeping proper form on figures, though, proves to be easier said than done. Most horses, like humans, will shift or cant their bodies slightly while traveling in order to modify an exercise to make it more accessible or easier given their asymmetry. Most frequently this appears on circles where the horse either bulges out on one side of the figure or collapses one side.

Here is a simple exercise for ensuring that you are getting the gymnastic benefit from your circles by keeping your alignment. It works by creating activity in both of the horse's hind legs, using a quick direction change *before* he can misalign his posture. This keeps him using both sides of his body, becoming more symmetrical. This exercise also tests responsiveness while it supples your horse's back and hind limbs.

Helpful Hint

★ Be sure to get a clear response from his hind end. You should not need to guess whether he has responded. If you are not getting a clear response from his hind end, use a whip to enforce your leg. Alternatively, it might be necessary to tune up your horse from the ground with the same exercise before trying it under saddle.

1 Begin in a working walk, making a 10-meter circle to the right.

2 With your right leg and while restraining the outside rein, ask your horse's haunches to yield to the outside of the circle. His hind legs will be walking a larger circle than his front legs.

3 At the centerline, change direction and bend.

4 Make a small circle to the left, again asking his haunches to yield to the outside.

5 Repeat the exercise going to the right.

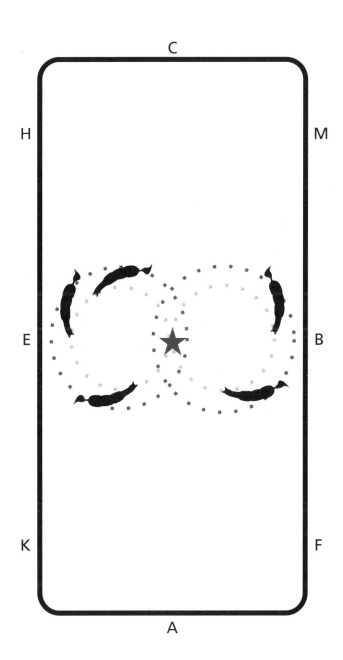

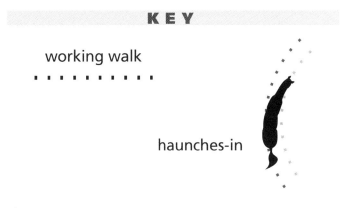

KEY

working walk

· · · · · · · · · ·

haunches-in

8. Circle Prep

LEVEL: INTERMEDIATE

BENEFITS

Using a circle to prepare for haunches-in allows the horse to develop lateral work fluidly, which means he doesn't stall out or leave his hind legs behind him. This exercise helps generate forward energy while shaping his bend and increasing the weight on his hindquarters before moving to haunches-in. It also ensures that the rider is developing an inside bend throughout the horse's spine rather than just shoving his hind end away from her outside leg.

Helpful Hints

★ The 10-meter circle is used to prepare and set up for haunches-in. If you do not get good bend and rhythm on the circle, your haunches-in will not be successful.

★ Keep your outside leg positioned behind the girth. Think about energetic but controlled rhythm.

1 Begin at **A** in a working walk.

2 At **F**, ride a 10-meter circle.

3 At the end of your circle, ask for haunches-in.

4 Proceed straight ahead in haunches-in.

5 At **M**, straighten your horse.

6 Repeat the pattern in the opposite direction. When mastered at the walk, ride the same pattern in both directions at a jog.

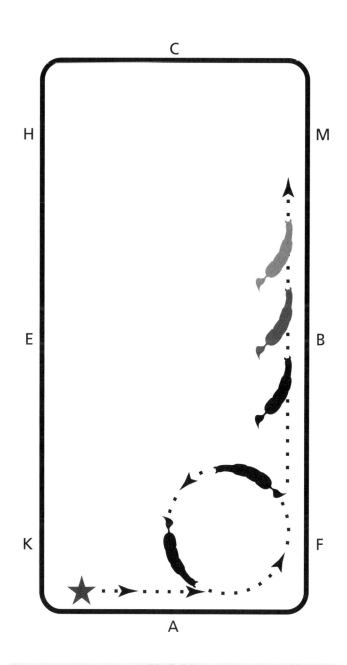

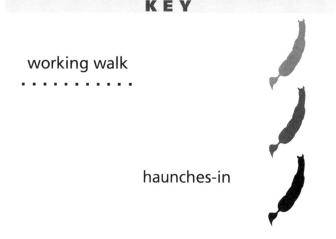

KEY

working walk

• • • • • • • • • • •

haunches-in

9. Lope Chute

LEVEL: **BEGINNER**

BENEFITS

This exercise prevents the common problem of horses getting crooked or leaning to one side in lope transitions. It also helps riders execute much more accurate lines in the lope by being accountable to a focal target. Riding accurate lines allows you to become much more adept at lead changes. This exercise also enables riders to feel subtle misalignments in the lope.

Helpful Hint

★ **Look up and aim for your gates!**

1 Set up three pairs of cones to create "gates" on a diagonal line as shown. Each gate is 3 feet wide.

2 Begin at **A** in a working lope, left lead.

3 At **F**, cross the diagonal through the first gate.

4 Before the middle gate, transition to a jog and proceed through the second gate.

5 After the middle gate, pick up a right-lead lope.

6 Pass through the third gate at a lope and track right at **H**.

7 Repeat this in both directions.

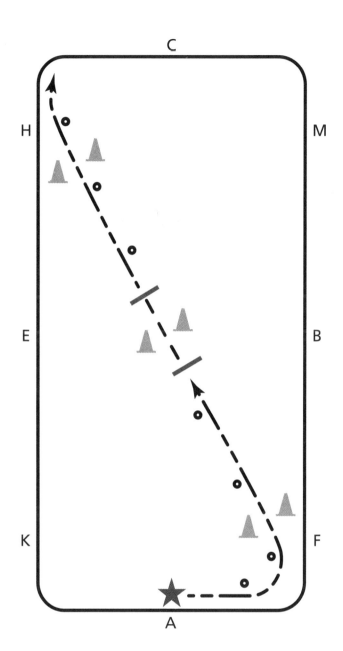

K E Y

working jog

— — — — —

working lope

— — ○ — — ○ —

cone ▲   transition ▬▬▬

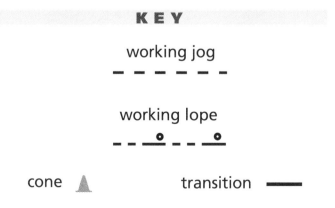

10. Box Turns

LEVEL: **INTERMEDIATE**

BENEFITS

Many riders have no idea how much sharper their horses could be to their aids until they ride this exercise. Turning inside a box and executing transitions precisely often helps fine-tune the timing of aids and the response from the horse. Remember — the quicker and more pliably our horses respond to our cues, the less often they plod around on the forehand!

Helpful Hint

★ This exercise requires your horse to be very responsive to transitions and turning cues. If you are hitting poles or are late on transitions, practice responsiveness by riding turns on the forehand, rein-backs, and halt transitions.

1 Set up a box with four 8-foot poles on the centerline as shown. Begin at **A**, and jog down the centerline toward the box.

2 Just before the box, transition to a walk. Enter the box, and halt.

3 Turn around inside the box without touching the poles.

4 Exit the box at a walk, the same way you entered.

5 Pick up a jog, and return to **A**.

6 Repeat the pattern numerous times, alternating the direction of turn.

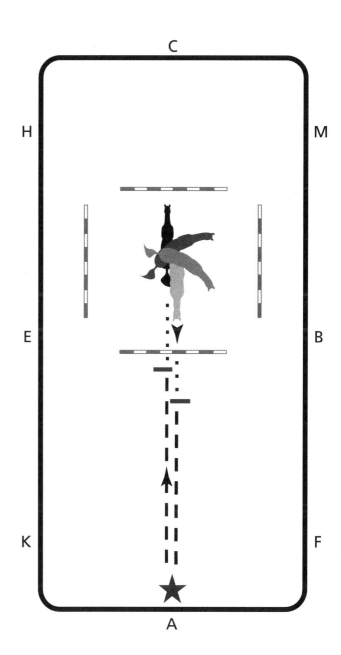

KEY

working walk · · · · · · · · · ·

working jog – – – – –

ground pole

transition

11. Testing Balance #1

LEVEL: INTERMEDIATE

BENEFITS

Sideways rotation of the hind legs in addition to deep flexing of the hind joints helps release tension that accumulates in the lower backs of performance horses. The movement also creates positive tension in the oblique muscles that assist in raising and supporting the back. In addition to physiological benefits, turns on the forehand help maintain the utmost responsiveness from our mounts.

This is an excellent exercise for horses that are dull to the rider's leg, requiring heavy or strong cues to move them sideways. By executing turns on the forehand, you can get your horse "tuned up" to your leg and then can use lighter cues for the rest of the session. This helps the horse do more of the effort of carrying himself in balance, rather than relying on constant aids.

This exercise is particularly useful because it blends the sideways crossing movement with forward energy. In between each turn on the forehand, you are able to refresh your horse's energy by moving resolutely forward. The exercise also tests whether the rider can ride nicely straight after the turn on the forehand maneuver, rather than getting overbent, crooked, or disorganized.

Helpful Hints

★ Most riders wobble off the centerline on this exercise. Pay attention and use your focal markers.
If you are struggling, add energy. It is always easier to hold your line with lively energy from the horse's hindquarters. If you lose impulsion or responsiveness from your horse, your centerlines will be very wiggly.

★ Take your time making the turns at each end, but ride a lively tempo on the centerlines.

1 Begin at **A**, facing down the centerline.

2 Proceed in a working jog down the centerline.

3 Before the end, halt.

4 Ride a 180-degree turn on the forehand.

5 Jog straight down the centerline back toward **A**.

6 When you get to your starting point, halt.

7 Ride another 180-degree turn on the forehand in the opposite direction.

8 Repeat the pattern, alternating the change of direction for each turn on forehand.

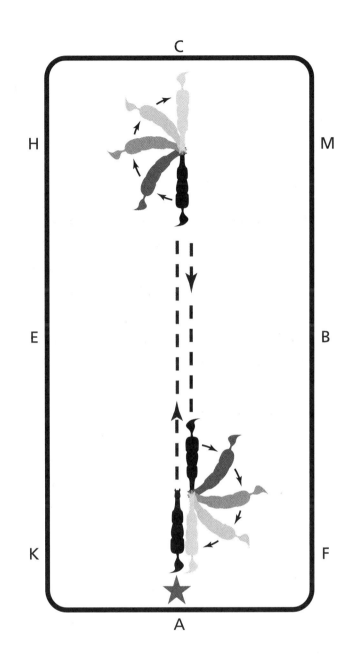

KEY

working jog

- - - - -

turn on forehand

12. Testing Balance #2

LEVEL: **INTERMEDIATE**

BENEFITS

Sideways rotation of the hind legs in addition to deep flexing of the hind joints helps release tension that accumulates in the lower back of performance horses. The movement also creates positive tension in the oblique muscles that assist in raising and supporting the back. In addition to physiological benefits, turns on the haunches help maintain the utmost responsiveness from our mounts.

This is an excellent exercise for horses that are dull to the rider's leg, requiring heavy or strong cues to move them sideways. By executing turns on the haunches, you can get your horse "tuned up" to your leg and then can use lighter cues for the rest of the session. This helps the horse do more of the effort of carrying himself in balance, rather than relying on constant aids.

This exercise is particularly useful because it blends the sideways crossing movement with forward energy. In between each turn on the haunches, you are able to refresh your horse's energy by moving resolutely forward. The exercise also tests whether the rider can again ride nicely straight after the turn on the haunches maneuver, rather than getting overbent, crooked, or disorganized.

Helpful Hint

★ Make your turns slowly at first, so your horse does not swing his haunches out but rather moves with his hind feet on the same spot.

1 Begin at **A**, facing down the centerline.

2 Proceed in a working jog down the centerline.

3 Before the end, halt.

4 Ride a 180-degree turn on haunches.

5 Jog straight down the centerline back toward **A**.

7 Before **A**, halt and ride another 180-degree turn on the haunches.

8 Repeat the pattern.

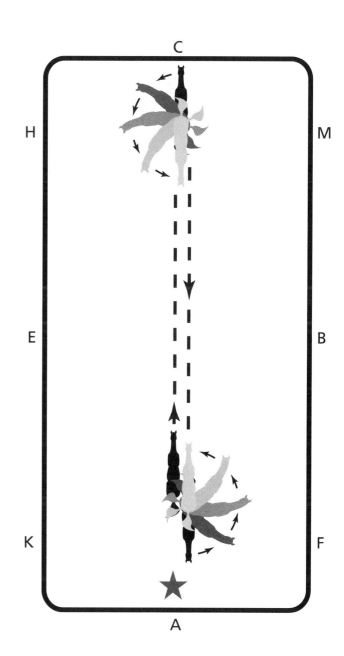

KEY

working jog

– – – – – –

turn on haunches

13. Leg-yield to Smaller Circle

LEVEL: **INTERMEDIATE**

BENEFITS

The ability to control placement of the horse's outside hind leg determines a rider's ability to create true collection. By shortening the outside of the horse's body posture rather than allowing it to get long and stretched out, you create a lope that is more upright and cadenced. This exercise helps you improve your horse's lope.

Helpful Hints

★ Do only four strides of yield-in. Many riders struggle with this exercise by trying to do too much.

★ If your horse sticks to your leg and does not move to a smaller circle, strengthen your request with a thump, then soften your request after getting a response.

1 Begin in a working lope, left lead.

2 At **C**, make a 20-meter circle. Lope the circle twice to confirm your rhythm.

3 As you pass **C** for the third time, use your outside leg to yield your horse in toward the middle of the circle for four strides.

4 Ride your horse back out to the 20-meter circle.

5 Each time you pass **C**, apply your outside leg for a leg-yield.

6 Repeat the pattern in the opposite direction on the right lead.

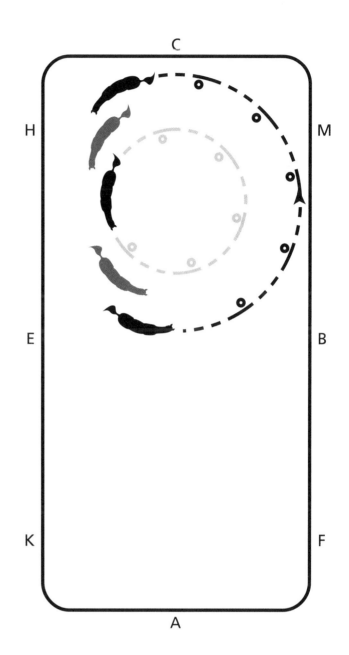

KEY

working lope

leg-yield
on a circle

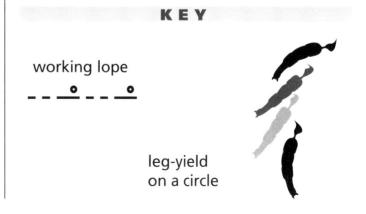

14. Lope Lightness

LEVEL: **INTERMEDIATE**

BENEFITS

By occasionally releasing rein contact when your horse is carrying himself well, you test his ability to balance himself fully for a moment, thus ensuring that he is not depending on your rein, leg, and seat cues. He should maintain the same tempo, poll flexion, and neck posture throughout. He should come neither behind nor above the bit. A version of this exercise has existed for years in dressage patterns as a way of testing the horse's thoroughness of training.

Helpful Hint

★ If your horse struggles with maintaining self-carriage in this exercise, try releasing just one rein at a time.

1 Begin in a collected lope, right lead. Ride a 20-meter circle at **E**.

2 As you cross over the centerline on each side of the circle, push your hands forward to put slack in the reins.

3 Ride for three strides with slack in the reins.

4 Develop your contact again with a soft feel of your horse's mouth.

5 Repeat the pattern in the opposite direction on the left lead.

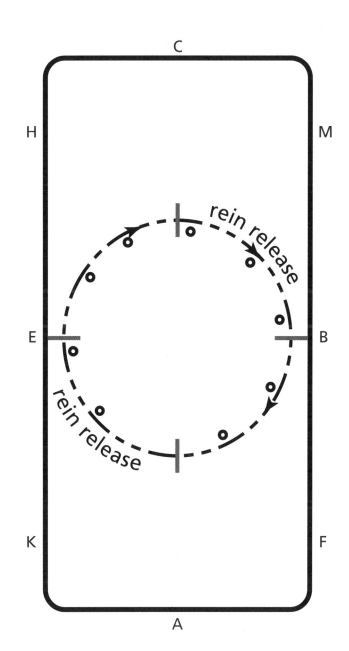

K E Y

collected lope

transition

15. Quarter Pirouette and Halt

LEVEL: **INTERMEDIATE**

BENEFITS

This exercise combines the benefits of hindquarter engagement with straightness and lightness by adding an immediate halt. This footwork prevents common mistakes when learning the pirouettes, including bracing the neck, falling sideways crookedly, or rushing forward. It is a great way to teach the initial working pirouettes.

Helpful Hints

★ Make your turn step by step.

★ If your horse moves too quickly or you use too much outside rein, he will flex incorrectly to the outside of the turn. Instead, you want him to remain flexed in his direction of travel. It is more important to emphasize this point when training him than to keep his hind legs nailed to a single spot on the ground.

1 In a collected walk tracking right, shorten your horse's steps before **C**.

2 Simultaneously, ask your horse to flex his head to the right.

3 Bring your outside leg back to hold his haunches in place and ask him to make a quarter pirouette.

4 When you arrive at the centerline, immediately halt.

5 Your halt should be straight on the centerline. In the halt, maintain flexion to the right. Look for your horse to be soft and relaxed.

6 Practice equally in both directions.

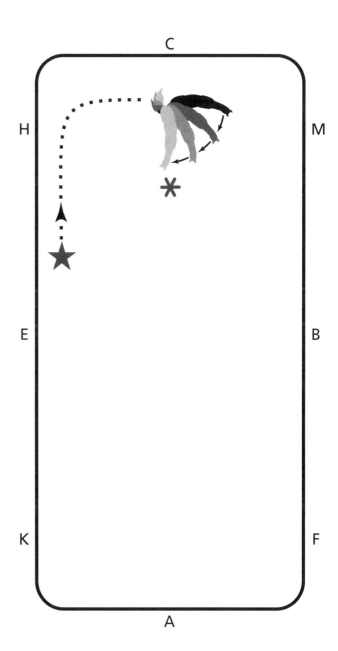

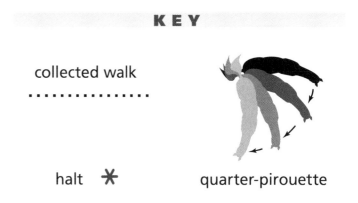

KEY

collected walk
· · · · · · · · · · · · · · ·

halt ✶

quarter-pirouette

16. Fine Tuning

LEVEL: **ADVANCED**

BENEFITS

A well-balanced horse is often said to be "between the rails" at all times, meaning he carries himself perfectly straight between the rails of the rider's legs, neither bulging to one side nor using his hind legs unequally. This exercise is a way of consistently putting him between the rails by clearly alternating the use of each one.

Helpful Hints

★ Take your time! There is almost no such thing as taking too long to do this exercise.

★ Be sure your horse is making each kind of turn accurately. Remain clear with your aids. Don't get sloppy.

★ If your horse gets confused or balky, dismount and practice this exercise from the ground.

1 Set up four cones as the corners of a square, with 15 meters between each cone, as shown. At a working or collected walk, ride a large box just outside the cones.

2 At each cone, halt.

3 Alternate riding turns on the forehand and turns on the haunches at each corner.

4 If your horse gets antsy anticipating the turn, skip the lateral steps, ride normally around the corner, and proceed to the next corner.

5 Repeat the pattern in the opposite direction.

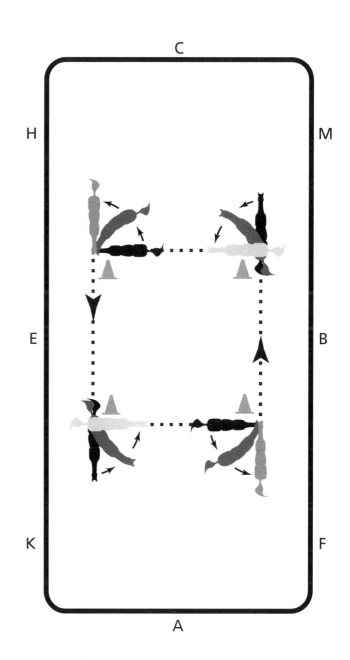

KEY

collected walk ············· cone ▲

turn on forehand turn on haunches

17. Half-pass to Leg-yield

LEVEL: **ADVANCED**

B E N E F I T S

This exercise is a nearly fail-safe method for ensuring the horse remains properly bent in half-pass. It works because the horse begins to anticipate the leg-yield, thereby keeping himself bent around the rider's inside leg during half-pass.

Helpful Hints

★ Keep your right seat bone and stirrup weighted throughout this exercise, in both the half-pass and the leg-yield.

★ Be sure to begin the half-pass with adequate energy.

★ If you feel ambitious, you can also ride this exercise at a lope.

1 Begin at **A** in a working jog or walk, tracking right.

2 At **K**, establish bend to the right and half-pass right four to five strides.

3 Straighten your horse and proceed straight ahead for 5 meters.

4 Establish right flexion and leg-yield left.

5 Repeat the pattern in the opposite direction.

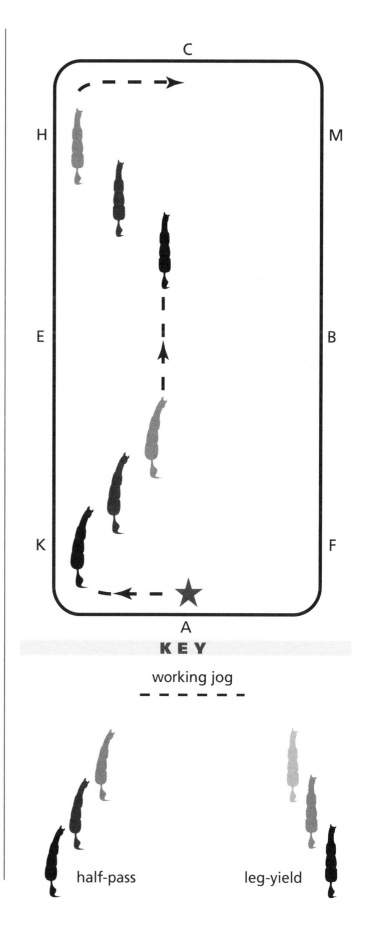

KEY

working jog

half-pass   leg-yield

18. Shoulder-in to Haunches-in

LEVEL: ADVANCED

BENEFITS

In addition to its strengthening benefits, this exercise is a good test of how your training in lateral work is progressing. By assessing how energetically and smoothly your horse is able to transition between these two movements, you can gauge whether he can move ahead. When he does not struggle with this transition, he indicates that he is capable of working at a higher level of collection in his general training.

Helpful Hints

★ Think of the 10-meter circle as a chance to refresh your horse's energy, as the lateral work will tend to sap it.

★ Motivate your horse to go forward around the circle so that the transition to haunches-in feels smooth, not labored. When doing this exercise at a jog, resume posting rather than sitting if your horse loses energy. This will help free up his back and create a surge in movement.

1 Begin in a collected walk or jog, tracking left.

2 Ride deep into the corner before **F**. From **F** to **B**, ride shoulder-in.

3 At **B**, ride a 10-meter circle.

4 Maintain the left bend from the circle and immediately ride haunches-in down the rail.

5 Ride haunches-in to **M**, straightening your horse before the corner.

6 Repeat the pattern in the opposite direction.

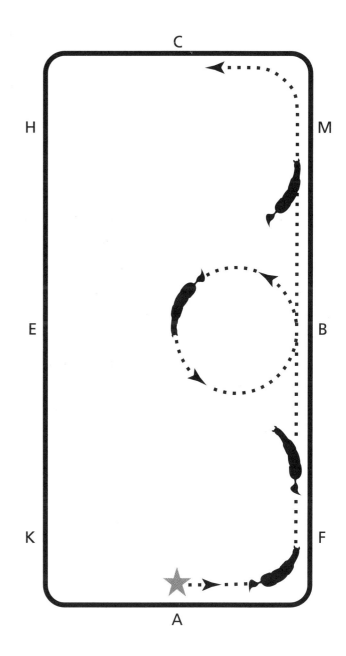

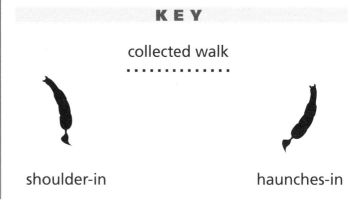

KEY

collected walk
· · · · · · · · · · · · ·

shoulder-in   haunches-in

19. Two Circles at Once

LEVEL: **ADVANCED**

BENEFITS

Think of this exercise as a side abdominal crunch for your horse. Essentially, you are asking him to support his posture while shortening the inside of his body and lengthening the outside. This tones all the muscles involved with hip stability, spinal flexion, and croup engagement.

It also makes the horse nicely malleable around the rider's legs. Remember that in Western Dressage one of the goals is to create a highly maneuverable horse. This exercise is sometimes a precursor to pirouettes.

Helpful Hints

★ Keep your pelvis aligned with your line of travel relative to your horse's shoulders.

★ Do not lean to the outside. If you struggle with this pattern initially, confirm haunches-in on a straight line before you attempt it on the circle.

★ Be sure your horse remains flexed to the inside at his poll.

1 Track right on a 10-meter circle at **E** in an energetic, marching walk.

2 Sit a little deeper on your inside seat bone. Press gently with your inside leg at the cinch to keep your horse's shoulder on the 10-meter track.

3 Draw your outside leg back behind the cinch and ask his haunches to step toward the middle of your circle.

4 Keep walking like this, maintaining energy. Ideally his haunches should walk on an 8-meter circle while his shoulders and front legs remain on a 10-meter circle.

5 Repeat the pattern in the opposite direction.

6 Once mastered, practice this exercise on a 20-meter circle at a jog in both directions.

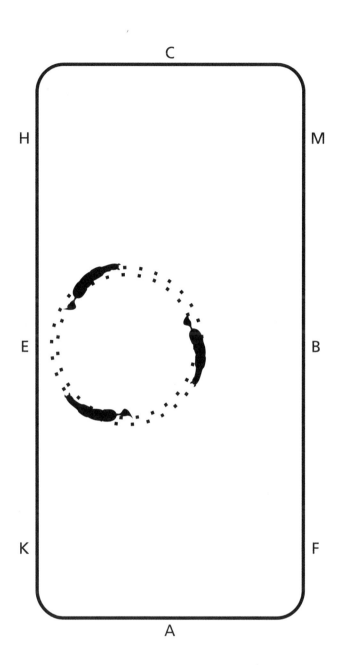

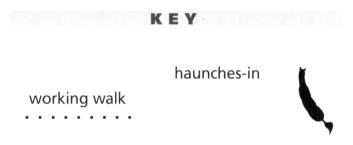

KEY

haunches-in

working walk

· · · · · · · · ·

CHAPTER 3

LOOSENESS

THE CORNERSTONE of any aspiring dressage rider's skills is the ability to ride "long and low," meaning to stretch the horse's topline forward and downward into the contact on long reins. This posture ensures that the horse is working correctly from his back and haunches. It also maintains looseness in the horse's shoulders, spine, and neck.

Unfortunately, many riders, aspiring to ride their horses on the bit, fail to realize that riding long and low is a critical component of riding a horse correctly into the contact. It often seems fashionable for riders to have their horses prematurely elevated and high-headed in an attempt to achieve collection.

The common result is a horse that appears to be on the bit while actually carrying his back and topline hollow, because the rider is trying to get the horse on the bit by shortening his neck and bringing his chin back. Moving exclusively in this false frame creates tension and stiffness in the spine. The goal should be to push the horse's whole body out to the bit, so that he lengthens and stretches his neck away from his chest.

Too often, riders think that an elevated head and neck position prevents the horse from moving with weight on the forehand. Lifting up the head and neck may give the false impression that the horse is now traveling uphill. In reality, his neck elevation has little to do with how much weight he carries on his forehand. It is very possible for a horse to have an elevated neck carriage and still be on the forehand.

This happens when the neck is elevated but not properly reaching forward and outward and therefore not recruiting the ligaments to lift and support the spine. This causes the hindquarters to push out behind the horse rather than up underneath him and places his balance on the forehand. Likewise, it is possible for a horse to travel with a low neck position and be *off* the forehand because he is engaging the important sling of thoracic muscles around his shoulder girdle that draws the weight up out of his front legs.

What to Focus On

Far more important than neck position are 1) looseness (not restriction) of the scapula and shoulder, 2) having the neck properly toned and not tense, 3) the lift and tuck of his abdominal muscles, and 4) the soft swinging of his back under the rider.

These elements directly determine whether a horse can elevate his withers and draw his weight up off his front legs. When one of them is not in place, the best plan is to ride in a long and low frame until it is corrected. Regardless of a horse's or a rider's level of training, riding in a long and low posture for a few minutes each day ensures the consistent quality of your ongoing training.

Just like their human counterparts, horses need frequent elongation of their spines. Some trainers refer to this as "opening" the back. Stretching the horse's spine from ear to tail releases potential rigidity and blockages before they can form. It relieves the pressure that builds up in the lower back due to collection, sitting jog, and other demands. Through its active stretching, riding long and low tunes up the strength and looseness of the horse's neck muscles, shoulder girdle, and pectorals. It maintains the suppleness — and therefore the performance — of these muscles in a way that is not accomplished when one rides only in a fixed and collected frame.

The Details of Long and Low

The correct neck position should be dictated by each horse's conformation. As a general rule, aim to ride with your horse's poll level with or slightly lower than his withers. You want him to extend his neck as if he were interested in sniffing something on the ground directly in front of him. Concentrate on maintaining positive but light tension in both reins equally and ride at the same tempo as for working jog, no faster and no slower.

If your horse raises his head and creates slack, shorten the reins quickly to maintain the positive but light tension. Once you have reestablished a feel of his mouth, begin to lengthen the reins again. When you are able to maintain a consistent feel with the contact by these subtle and quick rein adjustments, your horse will learn to stretch and hold a steadier posture in the long and low frame without becoming disorganized or lifting his head up away from the bit.

All horses respond to the rule that, without frequent loosening and elongation of the spine, a rider can only achieve a false frame. A horse that is allowed to stretch long and low as frequently as he travels in collection becomes looser, more content, better moving, and free of soreness day to day.

20. Controlled Wandering

LEVEL: **BEGINNER**

BENEFITS

Use this exercise as a warm-up to help your horse stay light and soft in his body, not looking to the reins for balance. It allows his joints the time they need to warm up and move through a full range of motion without restriction. This simple routine also gives both horse and rider a time to really *feel* and take stock of their bodies.

Helpful Hints

★ Remember to shift your weight to your inside seat bone each time you turn.

★ Use Sally Swift's Centered Riding technique of looking ahead where you want to go with soft eye gaze, rather than laser focus.

★ Be creative with geometry and try to fill every inch of your arena with hoofprints.

1 Before you begin your schooling session for the day, mount up and leave the reins long and loose.

2 Ask your horse to move forward at a working walk and initially allow him to go wherever he pleases.

3 Begin guiding him with minimal rein contact.

4 To turn left, take the slack out of the rein and tip your horse's nose to look where you want him to go. Then release the rein and allow your horse to move toward the point with no rein contact.

5 Continue making loops and turns this way. This diagram is a sample pattern.

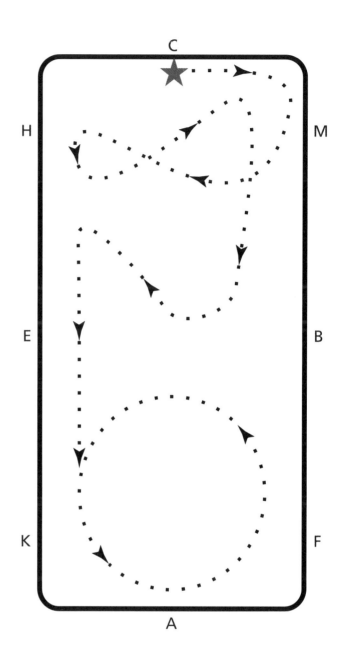

KEY

working walk

· · · · · · · · ·

21. Snake over Poles

LEVEL: **BEGINNER**

BENEFITS

Correctly bending a horse involves two variations of muscle recruitment. First, the muscles on the inside of the bend contract concentrically, which means they create strength by getting shorter. As the horse flexes his spine inward, the muscles of his topline and sides flex and shorten to draw his front and hind end closer together.

Meanwhile, the outside of his body needs to lengthen in order to allow the spine to bend. This engaging-while-lengthening type of muscle engagement is called an eccentric contraction; it governs collected movements. This exercise is so effective — yet simple — for developing this kind of strength that it is frequently used in physical therapy programs.

Helpful Hints

★ What matters most here are the horse's form and posture. While remaining on the bit, he needs to make each arc by flexing his spine, rather than throwing his inside shoulder into the turn and over the pole.

★ Be sure to close your new inside leg clearly for each bend.

1 Place two 8-foot poles end-to-end in the center of your arena.

2 In working walk or jog, ride a three-loop serpentine to cross over the poles.

3 Make your loops as wide as needed in order to create good bends without losing balance.

4 As your horse begins to change bends smoothly without hollowing his topline, make the loops tighter until you are barely riding out away from the poles.

5 Repeat the pattern in the opposite direction.

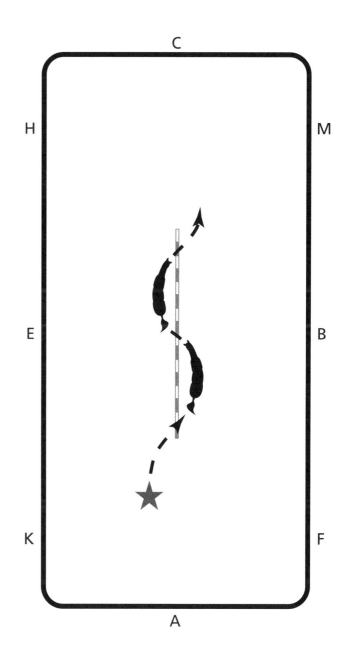

K E Y

working jog

– – – – –

ground pole

22. Circle Review

LEVEL: **BEGINNER**

BENEFITS

This exercise uses accurately ridden geometry to test your horse's flexibility. You want him to maintain the same cadence and frame on each of the different-size circles. Notice on the smaller circles if his jog maintains good swing or if he feels stiff and choppy. This will tell you about his flexibility. Accurately ridden figures are your most valuable training tool; this exercise sharpens your tools.

Helpful Hints

★ Don't rely on vague self-assessment for accuracy. Use cone markers or chalk on the sand. It is most helpful to ride this exercise after your arena has been newly groomed so that you can see in the sand how your geometry fares.

★ At the end of a properly ridden circle, your horse should feel rounder than at the beginning of the circle. Try to develop your feel for this.

1 Begin before **C** in a working jog, tracking right. Ride a 20-meter circle at **C**.

2 Proceed to **B** and ride a 15-meter circle.

3 Continue to **A** and ride a 10-meter circle.

4 If all went well, repeat the pattern in a working lope.

5 Repeat the pattern in the opposite direction at both a jog and a lope.

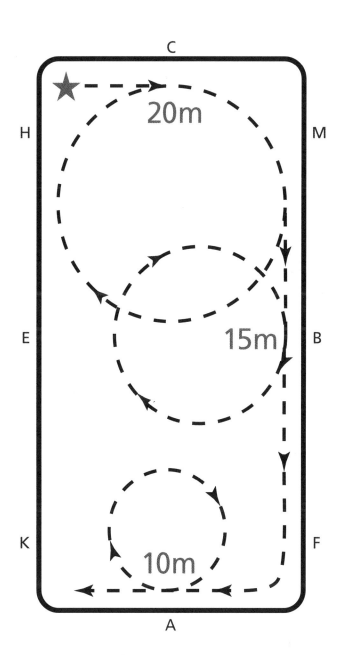

KEY

working jog

– – – – – – – –

23. Free Wheelin'

LEVEL: **BEGINNER**

BENEFITS

This exercise, though simple, is incredibly important for looseness and should be practiced frequently. In free walk, your horse should stretch through his neck, extending his nose ahead of the vertical while lowering his neck so his chin is level with or lower than his knees. By the end of this pattern your horse should travel with looser, more swinging strides. This motion through his back should move your hips more.

Helpful Hints

★ Ideally, in the free walk, your horse's back feet should step past the hoofprints left by his front feet. Imagine your horse walking with big steps like a prowling tiger.

★ To prevent your horse from lifting his neck in the turns, maintain energy and keep your hands low.

1 Beginning at **K**, develop a working or collected walk. Be sure to create lots of activity behind, as if ready to accelerate at any second.

2 At **F**, begin a shallow serpentine and develop a free walk by gradually allowing the reins to lengthen through your fingers a fraction of an inch at a time while maintaining a light contact. The reins should not become floppy or loose in free walk.

3 Continue through the short end and shallow loop on the opposite long side in a free walk.

4 Repeat the pattern several times in both directions.

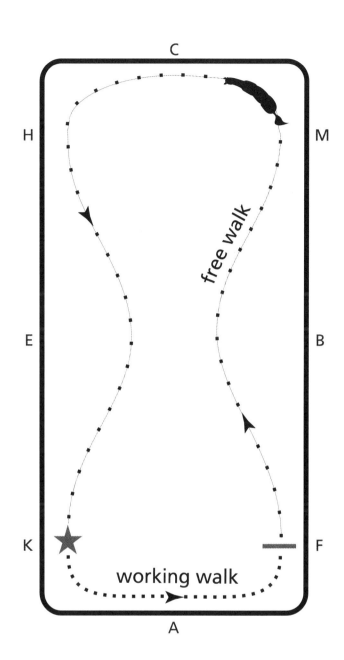

KEY

working walk   free walk

· · · · · · · · · · · ·   · · · · · ·

transition
—

24. Sit and Stretch

LEVEL: BEGINNER

Exercise scientists like Michael Weishaupt at the Sports Medicine Performance Center of the University of Zurich and veterinarian/author Dr. Gerd Heuschmann have shown in recent years that a horse absorbs motion through his back in a range of positive or negative ways, dependent on the elasticity and posture of his neck. Notably, the openings between vertebrae, through which nerves pass, are narrowed when he does not stretch and round his neck properly. Exercises like this one ensure that the rider controls the horse's correct neck elongation and opening of the back.

Helpful Hint

★ Reminders for how to "close" your seat around the horse to tell him to stretch downward (this is sometimes called "chewing the reins"):

- Roll your thighs inward.

- Close your lower legs on your horse's sides.

- Push the floor of your pelvis down as though clearing your throat.

- Push your elbows down to the ground.

- Gently squeeze and release the reins with your fingers to create a tiny vibration in the reins that your horse will feel at the corner of his lips.

1 Ask your horse to make a balanced halt while remaining on the bit.

2 If his hind legs are out behind him, ask him to take a half-step forward so that he stands with his weight evenly distributed over all four legs.

3 Without moving forward, ask him to lower his neck forward and down as if he were going to sniff something on the ground in front of him. To help him, wrap your legs around him in a hug with your weight seated deeply, chest lifted, and fingers very gently squeezing and releasing the reins like a sponge to create a tiny vibration at the corners of his lips.

4 Release the reins and praise him.

25. Warm-up Figure 8

LEVEL: **BEGINNER**

BENEFITS

This exercise maintains looseness in your horse's back, neck, and hips. Especially for Western horses that spend a lot of time in a collected frame and making powerful movements from their haunches, it is crucial to stretch downward for a period every day.

Helpful Hints

★ Remember to keep your upper body position tall and abdominal muscles toned. Look well ahead with your eyes.

★ Maintain a steady unchanging rhythm throughout the entire pattern.

1 Begin by riding a 20-meter circle at **A** in a working jog. Ask your horse to stretch forward and down into long (not loose) reins.

2 When you can make a complete 20-meter circle without losing this frame, shorten the reins and cross the diagonal from **K** at a working jog.

3 Ride a 20-meter circle at **C**, asking for the same stretching frame in the new direction and crossing the diagonal at **H**.

4 Repeat the whole pattern for at least 5 minutes.

Aim for this posture in the stretching jog.

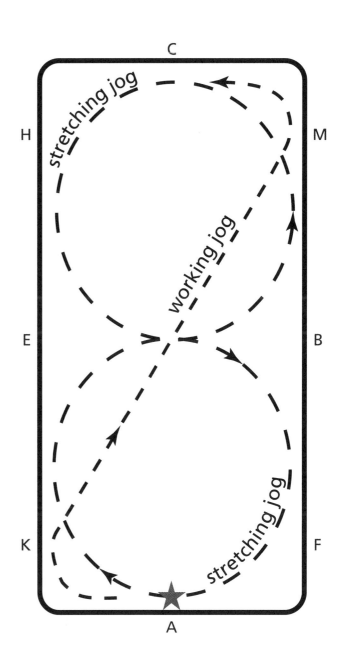

K E Y

working jog

– – – – –

stretching jog

– – – –

26. Stretching and Rounding

LEVEL: INTERMEDIATE

BENEFITS

The alterations in body posture called for in this exercise create more space between the horse's vertebrae and maintain looseness in the supporting tissue around his spine. This allows the motion of his hind legs to swing through his back smoothly.

Helpful Hints

★ Be sure to maintain a steady tempo when asking your horse to stretch down. Many horses try to rush, while others slam on the brakes.

★ If your horse is reluctant to stretch, it indicates that he is not working over his back in the working jog. To remedy, try some speed changes within the jog followed by figure 8s or serpentines to bend him.

1 Begin in working jog, tracking right.

2 At **E**, make a 20-meter circle, maintaining the same rhythm.

3 On the circle, gradually lengthen your reins, asking your horse to stretch his neck forward and downward toward the ground.

4 Ride a full circle in this stretched posture.

5 Gather your reins back up and ride a circle in a working jog.

6 Ask your horse to stretch down again.

7 Alternate riding circles in the two different frames and in both directions.

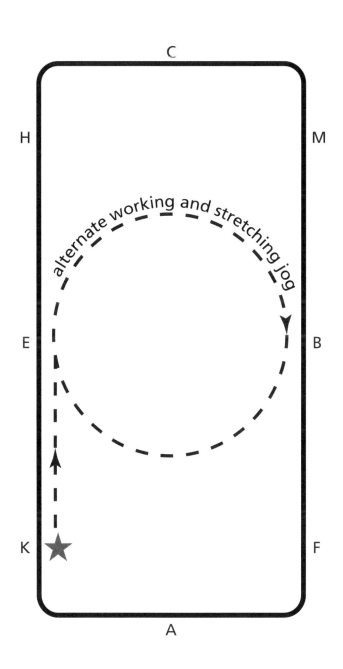

Aim for this posture in the stretching jog.

27. Cavalletti Half-circles

LEVEL: **INTERMEDIATE**

BENEFITS

The muscles used on the outside of the bend play a stabilizing role during many maneuvers in dressage. They support the spine and provide lateral balance to the horse so that he can properly recruit the muscles needed for good bending lines: internal and external oblique, rectus abdominis, transverse abdominis, latissimus. This exercise builds strength in these muscles.

Helpful Hints

★ If your horse hollows his back when crossing the poles, try posting rather than sitting the jog.

★ Encourage him to keep his neck low when crossing the poles.

★ Notice if one direction is smoother or easier than the other. If one side seems more restricted or unbalanced, leave the pattern for a moment of nicely energetic jogging and loping around the arena, then resume the pattern.

1 Set up two sets of ground poles along the rail in a fan shape as shown. Space them for your horse's jog stride (about 3 feet, 6 inches to 4 feet apart from the center of the poles).

2 Begin in a working jog and proceed in a half-circle left over the first set of poles.

3 Loop to the right to change direction and make a half-circle over the second set of poles.

4 Repeat. Be sure to change your bend for each half-circle and look ahead to cross the middle of the poles, not the outer edges.

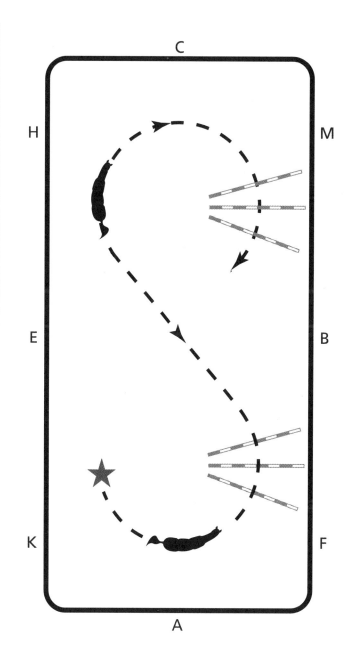

KEY

working jog

- - - - - -

ground pole

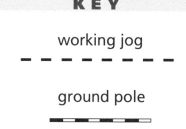

28. Suspension Square

LEVEL: INTERMEDIATE

BENEFITS

Horses' bodies are very similar to our own, in that continually making repetitive movements at the same rate of effort while maintaining a static body posture generally causes more harm than good. One frequent result, especially in the diagonal movement of jogging, is a spine that becomes as rigid as a rod.

The vertebrae brace closer together and lose their undulating mobility. The muscles that stabilize the spine constrict, reducing blood flow. This leads to further tension and stiffness over time, impairing the horse's ability to produce the freely flowing, springy, supple gaits we all strive for.

To prevent this scenario, make strategic adjustments to the horse's tempo, as in this pattern, which helps your horse develop more suspension while collecting his stride. This exercise not only loosens up your horse but can give a little spark to horses that have been drilled extensively in the arena. Consider it prevention of dullness.

Helpful Hint

★ Practice this exercise in both a sitting jog and a rising jog, to refresh your horse's forward energy.

1 Set up two poles at the bend of each corner on a large square. Place them at the appropriate distance for your horse's jog stride (about 3 feet, 6 inches to 4 feet apart at center).

2 Proceed in a working jog around the square.

3 Before each corner and pole set, flex your horse more to the inside and apply your inside leg at the cinch to develop bend.

4 Be sure to ride away from the second pole, heading straight toward the next corner and pole without wobbling.

5 Repeat the pattern in the opposite direction.

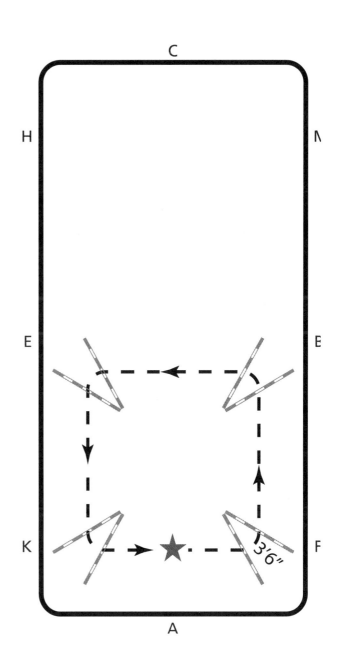

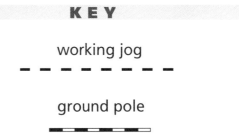

KEY

working jog

- - - - - -

ground pole

29. Testing the Walks

LEVEL: **BEGINNER**

BENEFITS

The horse's ability to change topline postures smoothly and without resistance tests and hones his balance and muscular pliability. With adequate longitudinal balance and loose spinal joints, a horse is able to transition back and forth between a working or collected frame and a longer stretched frame. When asked to do so, a supple horse will look like an accordion as his body posture lengthens and shortens without restriction. Being able to do this is a test of proper muscular development and a balance of strength between the flexion and extension chain of muscles.

This exercise helps achieve the balance and harmony between the muscles above and below the spine that govern the finely controlled, graceful movements we need for dressage.

Helpful Hints

★ In the lengthened and free walk, your horse's hind feet should step beyond his front hoof prints.

★ Keep your working or collected walk energized so that it feels like your horse is ready to accelerate at any second. If you find yourself "pumping" your seat almost every stride to motivate a lazy walk stride, throw in a few rapid walk-to-jog transitions to wake things up.

1 Begin at **H** in a working walk (or collected, depending on your level).

2 At **E**, turn onto the short diagonal and ride a lengthened walk, asking for maximum stride length.

3 At **F**, transition back to a working or collected walk.

4 At **K**, cross the diagonal in a free walk on a long rein. Your horse's neck should stretch out and down to the end of your reins.

5 Repeat the pattern in the opposite direction.

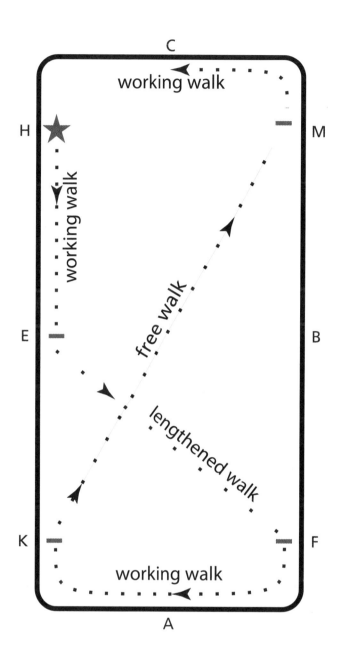

KEY

transition

free walk

working walk

lengthened walk

30. Adjust the Walk #1

LEVEL: **INTERMEDIATE**

BENEFITS

The motion of walking over poles creates movement through the spine — the same kind of looseness and swinging that a chiropractor will ask for when manipulating your horse. This wavelike motion maintains spacing between joints, which in turn allows the spine better flexion. It also causes the sacrum to rock gently side to side, which is incredibly valuable for relieving tension that builds in this area from the strains of performance.

When this tension is relieved, the horse's psoas muscles (a deep abdominal structure that rounds the horse's back and stabilizes his pelvis) are able to flex and stretch. This is arguably one of the most important determinants of how well a horse can perform.

Walking ground poles also helps maintain the purity of a horse's walk, especially for those that work a lot in collected gaits. These horses can build up rigidity in their backs, which will deteriorate the walk, causing it to become short-strided, tense, or pacelike. Ground poles maintain the rhythm and stride length.

While walking over a line of six to eight poles might seem too simple to be valuable, think again. Find a place on your property where you can leave these poles set up undisturbed and commit to walking over them 15 times before your training sessions. Notice any changes. Does the horse's back start to loosen up? Does his walk stride become longer afterward? Does he start to lower his neck?

Helpful Hints

★ Cue your horse with your seat to shorten or lengthen his stride in order not to bump the poles or add extra steps between them. If needed, practice some walk–halt transitions to get him on your aids.

★ Make sure that you keep a soft connection with the bit. Your elbows should be following the movement of your horse's mouth, even when crossing the poles.

★ Adjust the spacing and distance of poles as necessary for your horse's size. He should be able to walk comfortably over them without bumping.

1 Set up eight ground poles as shown: one set spaced 2 feet, 6 inches apart and one set spaced 3 feet apart.

2 Proceed in a marching working walk over the poles.

3 Shorten your horse's strides for the closer poles and extend the walk for the wider-spaced ones.

4 Ride over the poles like this several times in each direction.

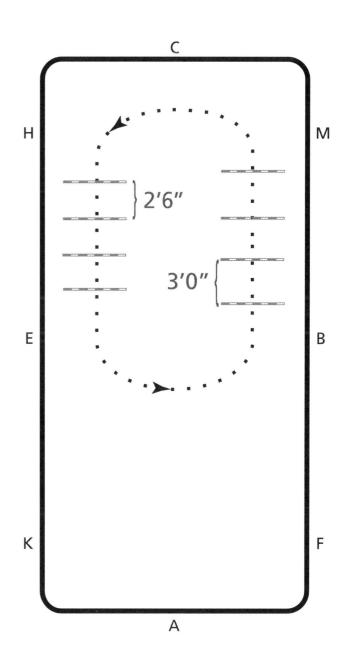

K E Y

working walk
· · · · · · · · ·

ground pole

31. Adjust the Walk #2

LEVEL: **INTERMEDIATE**

BENEFITS

The motion of walking over poles creates movement through the spine — the same kind of looseness and swinging that a chiropractor will ask for when manipulating your horse. This wavelike motion maintains spacing between joints, which in turn allows the spine better flexion. It also causes the sacrum to rock gently side to side, which is incredibly valuable for relieving tension that builds in this area from the strains of performance.

When this tension is relieved, the horse's psoas muscles (a deep abdominal structure that rounds the horse's back and stabilizes his pelvis) are able to flex and stretch. This is arguably one of the most important determinants of how well a horse can perform.

Walking ground poles also helps maintain the purity of a horse's walk, especially for those that work a lot in collected gaits. These horses can build up rigidity in their backs, which will deteriorate the walk, causing it to become short-strided, tense, or pacelike. Ground poles maintain the rhythm and stride length.

While walking over a line of six to eight poles might seem too simple to be valuable, think again. Find a place on your property where you can leave these poles set up undisturbed and commit to walking over them 15 times before your training sessions. Notice any changes. Does the horse's back start to loosen up? Does his walk stride become longer afterward? Does he start to lower his neck?

Helpful Hints

★ Cue your horse with your seat to shorten or lengthen his stride in order not to bump the poles or add extra steps between them. If needed, practice some walk–halt transitions to get him on your aids.

★ Make sure that you keep a soft connection with the bit. Your elbows should be following the movement of your horse's mouth, even when crossing the poles.

★ Adjust the spacing and distance of poles as necessary for your horse's size. He should be able to walk comfortably over them without bumping.

1 Set up eight ground poles as shown: one set spaced 2 feet, 6 inches apart on the ground and one set spaced 2 feet, 6 inches apart and raised 6 inches off the ground.

2 Proceed in a marching walk over the poles.

3 Be sure to stay in the center of the raised poles. Feel if your horse leans to one side or loses balance.

4 Repeat several times in both directions.

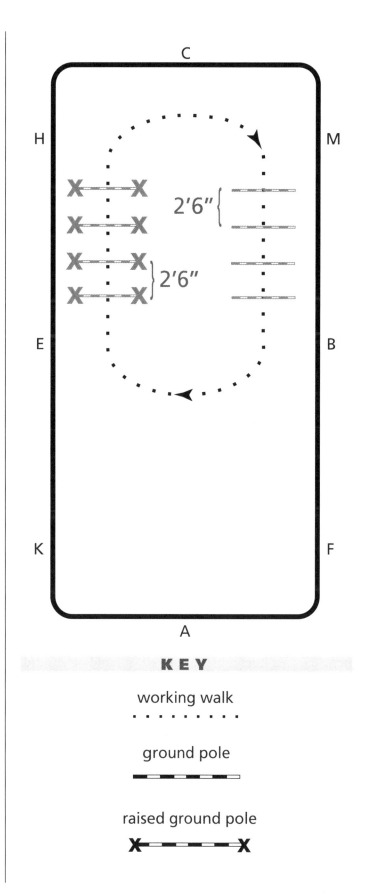

KEY

working walk
· · · · · · · · · ·

ground pole
▬ ▬ ▬ ▬ ▬

raised ground pole
X ▬ ▬ ▬ ▬ X

32. Raised Fan

LEVEL: **INTERMEDIATE**

BENEFITS

A horse's ability to use his hindquarters for engagement and propulsion depends not only on his hind legs but also on his front end. Before you look twice at this assertion, remember that the horse's entire trunk is suspended in a hammock-like sling of muscles and connective tissue. A fine network of muscles threads between the front of the rib cage, the neck vertebrae, and the scapulae.

These small but crucial muscles need to be both toned and elastic for the power of the hind end to be optimized. Without springy cushioned development of this region, the hindquarters will essentially be pushing energy forward into a rigid wall.

The fan exercise increases range of motion in both front and hind ends. When ridden consistently, it delivers measurable changes in your horse. It is also useful if, for some reason, your horse is not in a riding program at the moment. This exercise is equally beneficial for horses being worked in-hand or ground driving. It creates stronger stifles, supple and stronger oblique muscles (which bend the horse and support his trunk), and lighter forehand movement.

Helpful Hints

★ Keep your horse's spine bent in the direction of travel.

★ Maintain a slow, steady pace. The emphasis is joint flexion and finely controlled limb movements; this is not a speed exercise.

★ If your horse becomes anxious or starts knocking poles, increase the size of the circle until he can easily cope with the pole distance and height.

★ Use poles that are a minimum of 8 feet long; 10 to 12 feet is optimal.

1 Place four or five poles so they fan out and away from a central resting point on an overturned tub, stack of tires, or similar object approximately 1 foot, 6 inches tall.

2 Begin by riding your horse at a walk in a larger circle that includes only the outermost edge of the pole fan.

3 Gradually decrease the size of the circle toward the center of the fan. As the circle decreases the poles become closer and higher.

4 Practice five times in each direction.

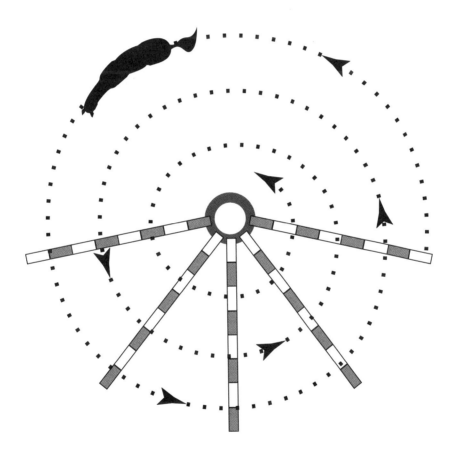

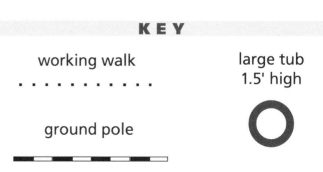

K E Y

working walk

· · · · · · · · · · ·

ground pole

large tub
1.5' high

○

33. Turn Both Ends

LEVEL: **INTERMEDIATE**

BENEFITS

When a horse finds bending in one particular direction more difficult than the other, it's common to assume a weakness resides on the side of his body placed on the inside of the bend at that moment. Many times this is not the case at all.

Very often, a horse struggles with bending maneuvers in the direction that places his weaker side on the *outside* and forces him to stabilize through eccentric contractions on the weaker side. Exercises that ask the horse to quickly alternate maneuvering one direction and then the other help resolve one-sidedness.

Helpful Hints

★ At first your horse might anticipate or become confused about which end you want him to turn. Make sure you clarify your aid and leg position to signal the different turns.

★ If you cannot tell which end is turning, ask a ground person to watch you.

1 Begin at **K** in a working walk.

2 At **E**, halt quietly.

3 Ride a 180-degree turn on the haunches.

4 Ride straight ahead in a working walk, bending nicely through the corner.

5 At **A**, halt.

6 Ride a 180-degree turn on the forehand.

7 Repeat in both directions.

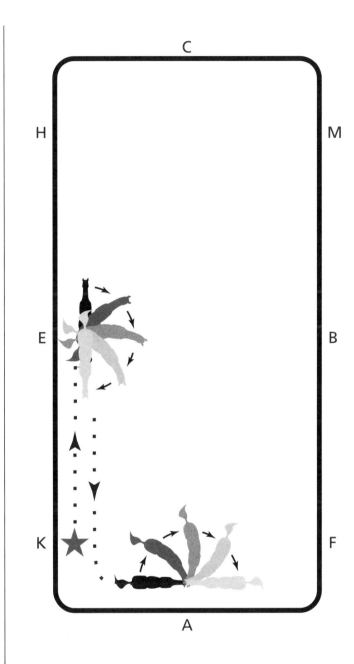

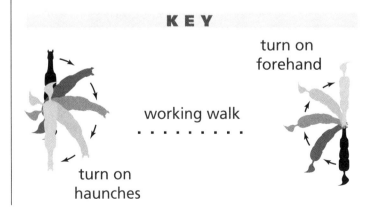

KEY

working walk

turn on haunches

turn on forehand

34. Jog Diagonals

LEVEL: INTERMEDIATE

BENEFITS

Using cross-rails to project the horse's energy over a balanced straight line helps him develop propulsive power in the hind end. Jogging over these small cross-rails also builds up the sling of chest muscles that play a critical role in cushioning and providing loft to his overall movement.

Helpful Hints

★ If your horse rushes, try riding over a single pole lying on the ground until he can approach, cross, and carry on without hurrying.

★ Keep your lower leg back underneath your hips.

★ Maintain a light feel of the reins, and do not push your hands forward over the cross-rail.

1 Set up an 18-inch cross-rail halfway across the diagonal.

2 Begin at **A** in a working jog.

3 Cross the diagonal at **K**, maintaining the same tempo.

4 Jog over the cross-rail and hold your line to **M**.

5 Ride a balanced corner.

6 Repeat the pattern at least five times.

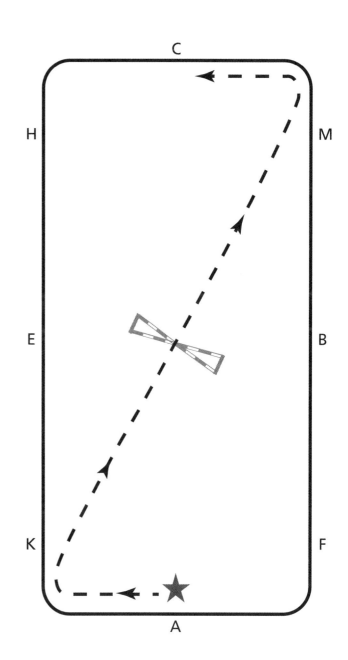

KEY

working jog

- - - - -

cross-rail

35. Three Step, Three Step

LEVEL: **INTERMEDIATE**

BENEFITS

This pattern tests and creates symmetry by increasing the horse's agility and the even use of both hind legs. It also helps riders gain control over their less dominant sides by aiming for an absolutely equal leg-yield response in both directions.

Helpful Hints

★ In this exercise you should take an equal number of steps sideways and straight forward. Many riders lose track of their sideways steps. Keep count and be accurate.

★ Using three strides at a time creates good stride control, so do not add more than this. Think of the straight-ahead steps as refreshing forward energy.

1 Begin in a working jog or walk.

2 At **A**, turn down the centerline.

3 Leg-yield from your right leg for three steps.

4 Ride straight ahead for three steps.

5 Leg-yield three more steps.

6 Again, go straight ahead for three steps.

7 Repeat this sequence until you reach the rail.

8 At **C**, turn down the centerline and repeat the sequence.

9 Repeat this exercise, leg-yielding from your left leg to the right.

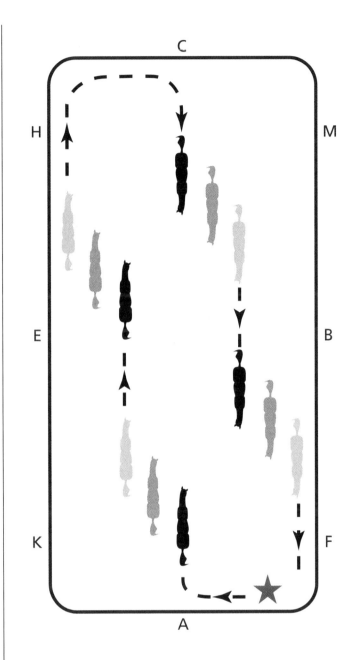

KEY

working jog

leg-yield

36. Leg-yield to Lengthening

LEVEL: **INTERMEDIATE**

BENEFITS

By immediately capitalizing on the suppling effects of lateral work, this exercise shows the horse how to express that looseness in a more extended stride before giving him time to fall on the forehand. Because of the accuracy and timing required of the rider's aids, this pattern is a good tune-up for riders wanting to compete in Western Dressage.

Helpful Hints

★ Keep your rein contact steady when you interrupt the leg-yield and ask for lengthening.

★ Ride a posting jog to encourage looseness in your horse's back.

★ If you are struggling at the jog, master this exercise first at the walk.

★ Be sure your horse comes back to a working jog tempo rather than rushing forward.

1 In a working jog, begin tracking right.

2 At **K**, leg-yield away from the rail, toward **X**.

3 After several strides, before **X**, straighten your horse on the diagonal line and transition to a lengthened jog.

4 Continue lengthening until **M**.

5 Transition back to a working jog.

6 Repeat the pattern in the opposite direction.

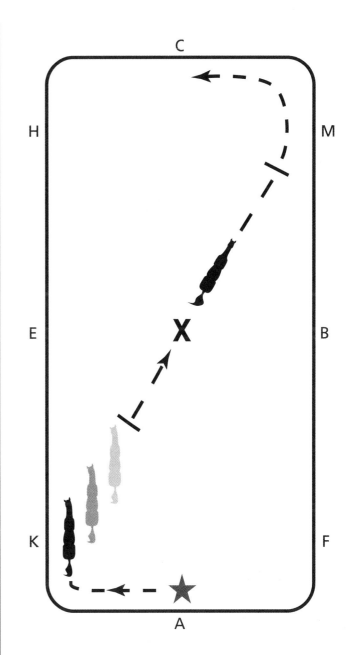

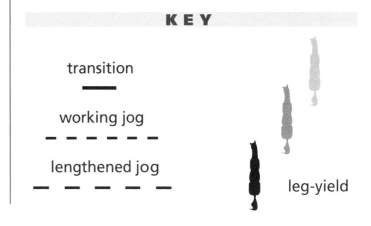

KEY

transition
——

working jog
– – – –

lengthened jog
— — — —

leg-yield

CHAPTER 4

RIDER DEVELOPMENT

ONE OF THE TRUE BEAUTIES of dressage is communicating with the horse through almost imperceptible cues. A good rider maneuvers her horse with subtle signals from her seat independent from rein use. The ability to use your seat this way elevates Western Dressage riding to an art.

With individual anatomical differences allowing for slight leeway from rider to rider, the general rules for a correct position in the saddle are as follows: When viewed from the side while mounted, the rider should demonstrate vertical alignment such that a plumb line can be drawn through the ear, shoulder, hip, and ankle. Sitting with the body or legs either ahead of or behind this vertical line most often indicates that the rider is out of balance with the horse, which interferes with his ability to use his hindquarters.

The rider should feel "plugged into" the horse's back with a firm, yet flexible stance. The posture is neither rigid and stiff, nor loose and too movable. Sound impossible? It's really quite simple.

The most effective way to find this balance is to stand in a martial arts posture called the Horse Stance because it is exactly the posture we adopt on horseback. Stand with your legs a little farther than hips' width apart. Bend your knees in a partial squat; angle your toes slightly inward; align your shoulder, hip, and ankle vertically; and point your tailbone straight down to the ground. Now, firm up your core, as if you were going to resist someone walking up to you and shoving you backward.

Notice how much weight bearing now falls on your upper and outer thigh muscles. Imagine being in this stance on your horse. This is commonly described as "riding from your core" because it requires toning up your abdominals and keeping your center of gravity low.

A stable dressage rider sits with exactly this same stance. You should feel not only firm but also light and easy for your horse to carry. In this posture your weight is evenly distributed on the three points of a triangle at the floor of your pelvis. These points are made of the two large seat bones easily felt when sitting on a hard surface and the front point of the pubic bone. To balance evenly on those three points, sit with your pelvis tipped neither forward nor backward. Some instructors tell students to imagine that the pelvis is a bucket full of water. To prevent water from spilling out, you do not want the bucket to tip either forward or backward.

One of the finer points of dressage — and a skill that most riders spend quite a bit of time mastering — is coordinating the energizing effect of the seat/leg in coordination with a slight passive restraint of hands that makes up the half halt. This cue helps the horse rebalance himself during moments when he might be putting too much weight on his front legs or otherwise falling out of balance. It is a subtle and complex request requiring exact timing and subtle application. It is also a skill that is very difficult to learn on one's own. Therefore, it's best to seek feedback from a skilled trainer on occasion.

The need for a particular position has more to do with function than aesthetic. Our goal is to allow the horse's back to be as unencumbered as possible. This is only achievable when our pelvis and joints are aligned to support our own weight while absorbing the horse's movement rather than sitting like a load that weighs down his spine. This alignment also allows us to cue the horse with subtle weight shifts and seat aids rather than pushing him around with our legs or heels.

37. Getting Centered

LEVEL: **BEGINNER**

BENEFITS

This exercise helps with balance and isolation. By removing leg contact with the horse's sides, it allows riders to feel where and how their seat bones are positioned. This is necessary for finding correct alignment. Doing this exercise, a rider can quickly assess if her tendency is to rock forward or backward on her seat bones.

Helpful Hints

★ Be sure not to tighten your buttocks or shoulders.

★ Keep your head balanced over your shoulders and look ahead with focused but soft vision.

1 With your horse standing in a square halt, drop your stirrups and your reins. (If your horse won't stand still, have someone hold him for you.)

2 Draw your heels up toward your buttocks, and hold them there for at least 2 minutes.

3 At the same time, open your arms out to the sides, straight out from your shoulders.

4 Keep your back flat, neither rounded nor arched.

5 Feel your hips dropping down into the saddle. Remain loose in your lower back and buttocks.

6 Once you are comfortable doing this at a halt, have someone lead your horse at the walk so that you can practice it while the horse is moving.

38. Rider Posture

BENEFITS

One of the quickest and most failproof ways to correct bad posture habits is with this exercise. Whenever a rider is not able to promptly assume and hold this position, it means she is habitually out of balance, most often with her legs too far in front of her seat.

Helpful Hints

★ With the correct leg position, you will be able to balance. If your legs are too far forward, you will tend to flop backward. If your legs are too far back, your chest will topple forward.

★ Keep your shoulders relaxed and your eyes forward. This is a good chance to feel for rider asymmetries. Assess whether you are leaning to one side when you stand in the stirrups or if one of your ankles wobbles or one of your arms tightens.

1 Ask your horse to stand quietly at the halt, or have someone hold him while you are mounted. Have your horse stand square and balanced with all four feet.

2 Drop your reins and allow your arms to relax at your sides.

3 If needed, draw your legs back to align your heels under your hips.

4 Keeping your knees slightly bent, stand up in your stirrups. Balance like this for several seconds.

5 For added challenge, extend your arms straight out in front of you, level with your shoulders.

39. Rider Coordination

LEVEL: **BEGINNER**

BENEFITS

This exercise makes riders pay attention to and readjust their bodies, both vital skills for dressage. It helps alleviate side dominance and postural habits such as collapsing a hip, dropping a shoulder, and the preference to ride one direction over the other.

Helpful Hint

★ It is helpful to have a checklist:

- Are my shoulders parallel to my horse's?

- Am I following the exercise correctly?

- Can I return to sitting jog softly without interrupting my horse's rhythm?

1 Begin at **F** in working jog, posting. Post on the outside diagonal.

2 At **K**, change to sitting jog and continue down the long side.

3 At **H**, resume posting. This time post on the inside diagonal.

4 At **M**, return to sitting the jog.

5 Repeat this pattern in both directions until it goes smoothly.

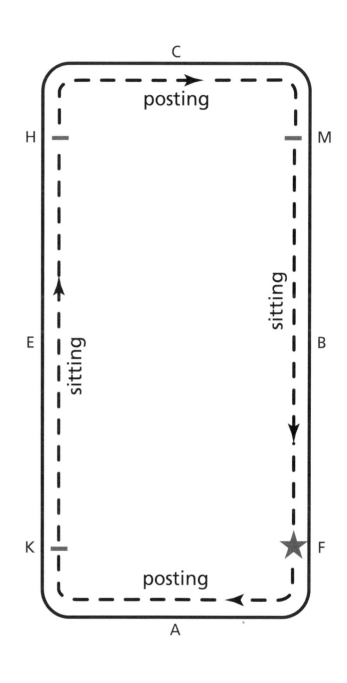

K E Y

working jog

– – – –

transition

▬

40. Independent Seat

BENEFITS

This maneuver places the rider in such a drastically altered position that it quickly fixes misalignments or poor habits. Furthermore, it precludes riders' tendency to be rein dependent.

Helpful Hints

★ Moving our arms like this makes us realize how much the rest of our body wants to tighten or lose balance.

★ Practice this exercise for short segments at first. Begin on a circle, and then work up to riding all the way around the arena.

1 Develop a working lope, tracking left.

2 Once you have established a good rhythm, hold the reins with your right hand while extending your left arm straight up overhead.

3 Maintain your rhythm and hold your line. Sit squarely and evenly in the saddle. Keep your shoulders level and relaxed.

4 As you reach up with your left arm, allow your hips to be heavy and sink deeper into your saddle.

5 Repeat, loping to the right and raising your right arm.

41. Finding Feel

LEVEL: **BEGINNER**

BENEFITS

In dressage the rider often must cue the horse's inside hind leg at various times. It is necessary to have precise timing. Revisit this exercise frequently to fine-tune your feel and timing, and don't be afraid to use mirrors or a ground person to verify you are feeling the right timing correctly. This exercise is a necessary precursor to riding lateral movements.

Helpful Hints

★ If you are not able to reliably feel your horse's inside hind leg coming forward and his rib cage swinging away from your leg, try this exercise without stirrups.

★ It is also sometimes easier to feel the inside hind leg on a smaller circle, so adjust as needed, perhaps using a turn on the forehand until you can reliably feel the inside hind leg.

1 Walk your horse on a light rein with just enough contact to steer him.

2 When comfortable, close your eyes for a few seconds as you walk. Try to feel when your horse's inside hind leg swings forward.

3 Do this a few more times.

4 Each time you feel that leg swing forward, give a gentle press with your inside leg.

5 Continue syncing your inside leg with the horse's inside hind leg.

6 Repeat in the opposite direction.

41. Finding Feel

42. Developing Seat

LEVEL: **BEGINNER**

BENEFITS

Good riders from all disciplines share something in common: they ride with a low center of gravity, sometimes called a deeply connected seat. It gives them the appearance of being plugged into the horse's back and makes their aids more effective. This exercise lets riders practice rotating their upper bodies while keeping their pelvis and waistline stable, necessary for developing a low center of gravity.

Helpful Hints

★ In this exercise, you're practicing alignment and sitting deeply. To facilitate this, remember to breathe in a full, relaxed manner.

★ Keep your abdominal muscles engaged, and align your arms to be relaxed and loose.

1 At a medium walk, stretch your upper body tall. Feel or look to be sure you have correct shoulder-hip-heel alignment.

2 Continue walking, and incline forward from your hips 45 degrees without rounding your back. Be sure to keep your legs in the same position, maintaining hip–heel alignment.

3 Return to center.

4 Recline backward 45 degrees, maintaining hip–heel alignment with your legs.

5 Return to center.

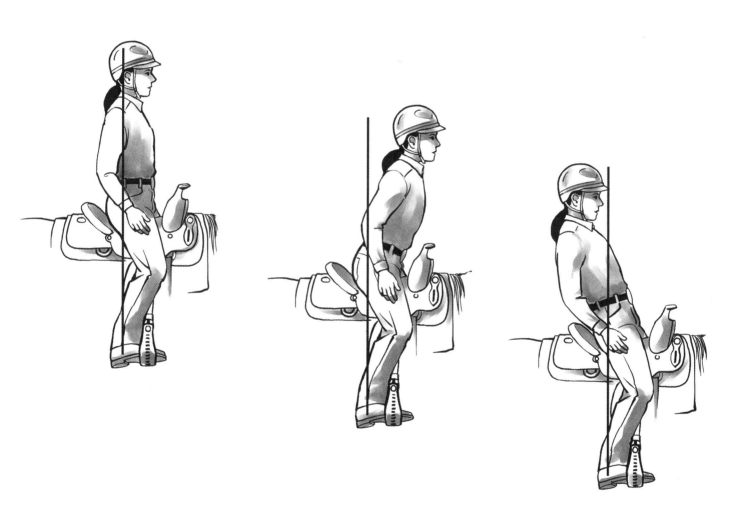

43. The 4x4x4

LEVEL: **BEGINNER**

BENEFITS

This exercise is more for the rider than the horse. It is useful for riders struggling with their leg positions or the effectiveness and clarity of their cues. Basically, it encourages the rider to *use* her legs instead of sitting passively on the horse. It has the side effect of opening the hips — something we all need! In addition, by moving around in the saddle, the rider is more able to isolate different body parts later in the ride.

You must begin this exercise with a good hip–heel alignment. Be sure that a plumb line dropped down from your hip would intersect your heel.

Helpful Hints

★ In the two-point position, balance your weight in your stirrups while carrying your seat just above the saddle. Stretch your upper body tall and keep your knees supple to absorb motion.

★ In all transitions, control your body to make smooth adjustments without disturbing your horse's balance.

★ Remember to give your horse clear guidance with steering (it is easiest just to follow the arena fence).

★ Do not flop down abruptly when you resume sitting jog; sit down lightly.

★ Stop and regain your hip-to-heel alignment any time you lose it!

1 Begin in a sitting jog. Establish a good working rhythm.

2 Proceed in a posting jog for four strides. (Count strides on the horse's outside shoulder. Each time it comes forward counts as one stride.)

3 Immediately hold yourself up in a two-point (half-seat) position for four strides.

4 Resume a sitting jog for four strides.

5 Maintaining a steady jogging rhythm, repeat entire sequence several times.

44. No Hands

LEVEL: **BEGINNER**

BENEFITS

This exercise mandates that you think and act first with your body. It prevents you from becoming rein dependent and helps you discover gaps in communication with your horse. Even if you feel you are not having much success at first, keep practicing.

Helpful Hints

★ If you are not at first successful, try riding this exercise at different times during your ride. Some horses will be more responsive at the end of a ride, for example.

★ *Progressively* decrease the amount of rein contact needed to stop your horse. It may take several repetitions of the patterns to eliminate any need for the reins.

1 Begin in a working walk with very light contact. Your horse does not need to be on the bit.

2 Ask your horse to halt by using only your seat, no reins. Let the energy out of your seat, freeze your hips and lower back, exhale, and think, "Whoa."

3 If your horse ignores you or gets confused, close your fist on the reins to enforce your seat cue.

4 Proceed at a walk, and again try asking for the halt with your seat only, no hands.

5 Practice to the point where you can stop your horse without touching your reins at all.

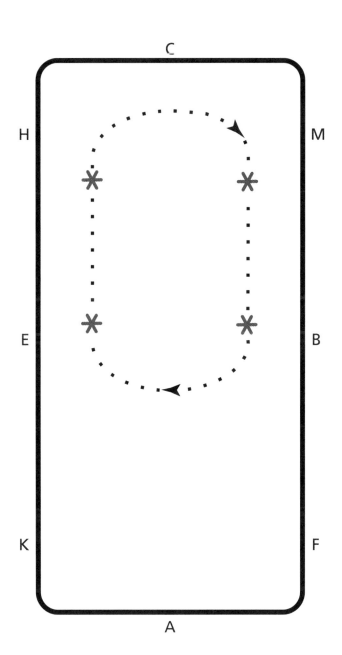

K E Y

working walk
· · · · · · · ·

halt ✳

45. Pelvic Rock

LEVEL: BEGINNER

This exercise helps the rider become more effective at riding the lope by practicing the mechanics of the pelvis necessary for developing collection. It helps you exert more influence over the lope stride, rather than becoming disorganized when the horse struggles for balance in the lope.

Helpful Hints

★ To ride the lope well, your pelvis must follow a rocking motion throughout the three beats of each stride. Your outside seat bone lands first, followed a split second later by your inside seat bone; then your inside hip swings forward.

★ It can be helpful to practice this motion unmounted while standing on your feet.

1 Develop a working lope, left lead, on a 20-meter circle.

2 Once you establish a consistent figure and rhythm, carry your reins in your left hand only.

3 Place your right hand, palm facing down, under your right seat bone.

4 On the first beat of each lope stride, press that seat bone down onto your hand.

5 Use that connection between your backside and your hand to keep yourself grounded in the lope.

6 Repeat the exercise in the opposite direction on the right lead.

46. Mindful Corners

BENEFITS

By riding a transition before each corner, you are prepared to really feel and influence your horse's bend. This prevents your horse from "freewheeling" through turns. It also helps you plan ahead and prepare your horse for movements.

Helpful Hint

★ In order to execute this pattern well, make sure your timing for the downward transition occurs well ahead of the corner. Do not wait until you are already *in* the corner to ask for the transition. Look up and ahead.

1 In the corner before **C**, begin in a working walk.

2 Ride a good bend and go deep in the corner.

3 After passing through the corner, transition to a working jog.

4 Before entering the next corner, transition back to a walk.

5 Again, bend and ride deeply into the corner.

6 After the corner, resume a jog.

7 Ride every corner this way for several repetitions in both directions.

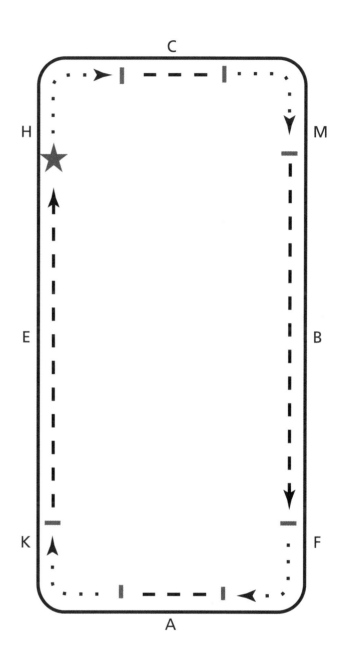

KEY

working walk

· · · · · · · ·

working jog

– – – – –

transition

▬

47. Lope Transitions on Centerline

LEVEL: **INTERMEDIATE**

BENEFITS

This exercise tests the clarity of your horse's responsiveness to your lope cue by asking for specific leads on a straight line. Confirm jog–lope transitions on bent lines and corners first, since these will confirm your horse's balance. Then tackle this straight-line exercise, which forces you to prepare for the lope by your seat alone without the help of a curved line.

Helpful Hints

★ If you have trouble, take a moment to reevaluate how you are asking for the lope. Chances are you might be doing too much (e.g., looking down at the ground, shaking your hands around, or drifting off your line).

★ As you ride down the centerline, prepare your horse by slightly flexing his poll in the direction of your desired lead; then ask for the lope.

1 From a working walk or jog, turn onto the centerline at **C**.

2 Once you are straight on the line, transition to a working lope, left lead.

3 Hold straight on your centerline. Before the end, transition back to a jog or walk.

4 Turn left at **A**, return to **C** and turn again onto the centerline.

5 This time, transition to a right lead lope.

6 Practice the pattern at least four times on each lead.

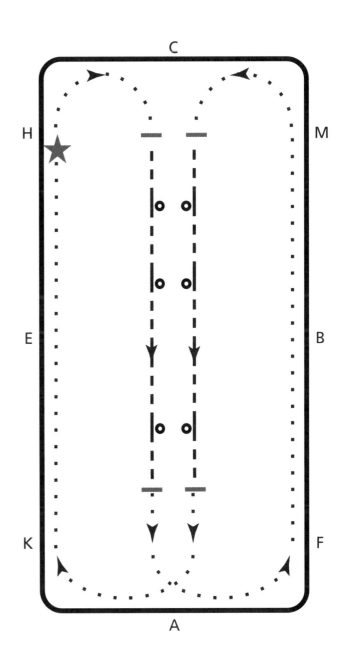

K E Y

working walk
· · · · · · · · · ·

working lope
– – o – – o

transition
▬

48. Box Transitions #1

BENEFITS

Most dressage exercises aim toward an elusively perfect execution, but sometimes when developing the horse's way of moving, we need to let things get a little messy. We need to create gaits that move smoothly through his body and choose patterns that cause our horses to be accountable for their own balance.

By asking a horse to think on his feet like this, we help him dissolve restrictions and stiffness that may be limiting him. He then gains agility and better symmetry between both sides of his body. Especially for horses needing to undo long-standing postural habits, change can happen quickly with such exercises as the square of ground poles in these Box Transitions routines.

Helpful Hint

★ This exercise has different components. Each time you ride it, choose one to focus on. For instance, the first time you ride through the exercise, think about making smooth, unrushed transitions between gaits where designated. The next time, concentrate on riding evenly sized arcs and good consistent bends. Another time, address the steadiness of your gaits, aiming for good rhythm with light contact.

1 Set up a box using four 8-foot poles as shown.

2 Starting from **K**, walk past the box.

3 Turn right and proceed over the middle of poles 1 and 2.

4 Transition to a jog, circle left, and cross the middle of poles 3 and 4.

5 Turn right in the jog and circle toward pole 3.

6 Before pole 3, transition to a walk, then cross the middle of that pole.

7 At the center of the box, halt.

8 Proceed over pole 4 to exit the box and repeat the pattern. Practice several times in each direction.

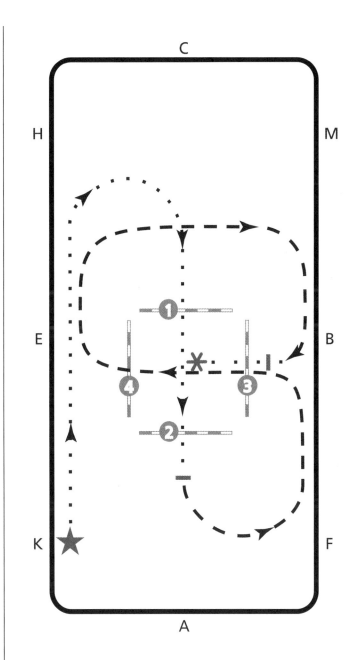

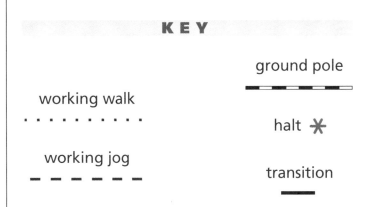

KEY

working walk
· · · · · · · · · · ·

working jog
– – – – – –

ground pole

halt ✳

transition
—

49. Box Transitions #2

LEVEL: INTERMEDIATE

BENEFITS

Most dressage exercises aim toward an elusively perfect execution, but sometimes when developing the horse's way of moving, we need to let things get a little messy. We need to create gaits that move smoothly through his body and choose patterns that cause our horses to be accountable for their own balance.

By asking a horse to think on his feet like this, we help him dissolve restrictions and stiffness that may be limiting him. He then gains agility and better symmetry between both sides of his body. Especially for horses needing to undo long-standing postural habits, change can happen quickly with such exercises as the square of ground poles in this and the previous routine.

Helpful Hints

★ You will need to collect and shorten your horse's lope stride in the center of the box so he does not rush or lose balance.

★ Be sure to keep your loping loops the same size.

★ Keep your eyes forward!

1 Set up four 8-foot poles as shown. Start in a working jog and proceed straight over poles 1 and 2.

2 Depart in a working lope, right lead, and circle right.

3 Lope over poles 4 and 3.

4 Circle right and lope over poles 2 and 1.

5 Transition down to a working jog.

6 Repeat the pattern in the other direction using the left lead lope.

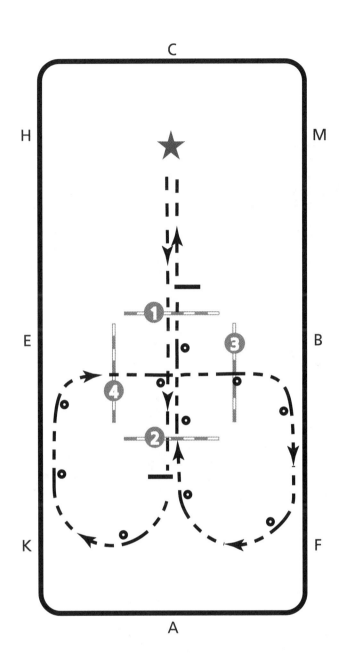

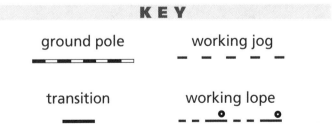

KEY

| ground pole | working jog |
| transition | working lope |

CHAPTER 5

ENGAGEMENT

ASK FIVE DIFFERENT TRAINERS to define engagement and you'll get five different answers. In all honesty, it's pretty tough to define this term concisely. In a nutshell, engagement describes how the horse uses his hindquarters when in motion. In dressage, we want his hindquarters and hind legs to demonstrate engagement, which is to say we want them to create the power that generates his movement, just like the motor on the back of a boat pushing it through water.

This is evidenced by the horse's whole hindquarters appearing to lower to the ground, as though preparing to sit down. The joints of his hind legs — hip, stifle, hock — also flex more (think of a human doing squats) when the horse is engaged. They should appear to be doing more work than the front legs. Otherwise, the horse is pulling himself forward by his front end — the opposite of what we want!

A horse moving with engagement travels with springy steps and the fluidity of a dancer, while one without adequate hind limb flexion and power moves without buoyancy. His steps seem weighted to the ground and are often short or choppy, toe-dragging, or lazy.

The exact definition of engagement taken from dressage judging glossaries is as follows:

> Increased flexion of the lumbosacral joint and the joints of the hind leg during the weight-bearing (support) phase of the stride, thus lowering the croup relative to the forehand ("lightening the forehand").

Engagement is carrying power, rather than pushing power. Note: Engagement is not exaggerated hock action (as seen most clearly in gaited horses and hackneys) in which the joints of the hind legs are most markedly flexed while the leg is in the air. Nor is engagement solely the length of the step of the hind leg forward toward the horse's girth.

A horse develops engagement over time. It requires that he build the strength and flexibility to lower his lumbar and sacral joints, which happens by his lifting and toning his abdominal muscles and carrying his rider easily. The best way to learn how to feel proper engagement, other than by riding a highly trained horse who can give you the right feeling, is first to learn to recognize it from the ground. Putting that visual together with what you feel when you are in the saddle will help immensely.

If you're fortunate enough to have a herd of young horses nearby, start to develop your eye by watching them move around. Notice how they move about with legs taking irregular lengths of stride, their bodies in no exact posture, their legs swinging freely without appearing to be making any effort.

Now contrast that movement with a horse being ridden in collected jog over a row of cavalletti. Watch this horse's rounded topline, how his haunches tuck under him toward the ground, and how his hind joints (hip, stifle, hock) flex more in order to propel his mass rhythmically over the poles in a finely controlled motion. This horse represents engagement, while the frolicking youngsters represent the total opposite. Learn to *see* engagement from the ground, and it will be much easier to *feel* from the saddle.

50. Circle Up

LEVEL: **BEGINNER**

BENEFITS

When a horse's neck, poll, jaw, or long back muscles are stiff, he is not able to execute small circles without quite a bit of struggle or resistance. This is often due to restriction or dominance in a muscle group as it needs to transition from an actively engaged role to a passively stretched and tensioned role. Practicing this exercise equally in both directions can alleviate this resistance.

Helpful Hints

★ Don't let your reins get too long.

★ Keep the same rhythm on your circles as you do on straight lines.

★ Watch your geometry. Make sure your 10-meter circles don't cross over the centerline.

1 Begin in working jog at **A**.

2 At **K**, **E**, and **H** ride a 10-meter circle.

3 Repeat at **M**, **B**, and **F**.

4 Once you have mastered the jog, ride in the pattern in the lope, adjusting circle size to 15 meters.

5 Repeat the pattern at both a jog and a lope in the opposite direction.

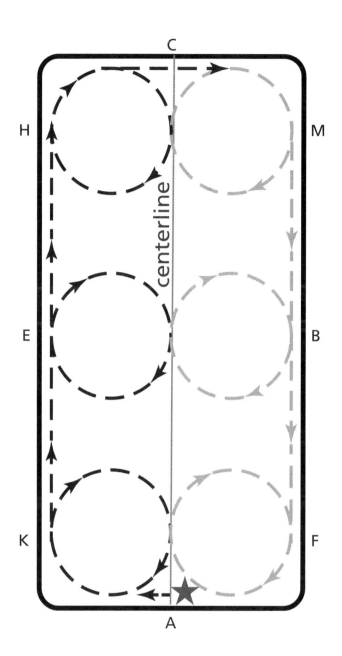

K E Y

working jog

– – – – –

51. Balance Pattern

LEVEL: **BEGINNER**

BENEFITS

A horse's suppleness and symmetry can be vastly improved by strengthening the muscles that stabilize his hip and stifle joints and his lower back. As a horse becomes stronger in these areas, his quality of bending in both directions will equalize. Not only will he be able to flex his spine and rib cage inward for a bend, but he will also be able to support his balance and movement by properly tensioning his outer body.

This exercise develops strength in the muscles around the horse's hips and stifles. It combines good joint flexion — caused by lifting the legs over poles — with stabilizing strength and balance from gait transitions.

Helpful Hints

★ Control your speed. Take your time.

★ With each repetition, the transitions to and from the lope should become smoother.

1 In the corner between **A** and **F**, set up four 8-foot poles in a fan pattern, spaced 3 feet, 6 inches apart at the center, as shown. Place another 8-foot pole across the track between **H** and **E**.

2 Begin in a working jog and proceed over the pole fan, crossing the center of each pole.

3 After passing the fan, depart in a lope, right lead.

4 Cross the single pole in a lope.

5 Return to a jog.

6 Repeat the pattern in both directions.

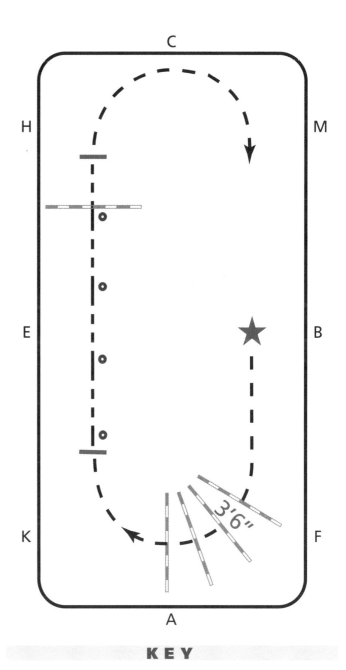

KEY

working jog

working lope

ground pole

transition

52. Over and Forward

LEVEL: **BEGINNER**

BENEFITS

This exercise addresses an issue most riders have with the leg-yield: the horse's disengaging and leaving his hind legs behind him. By accelerating slightly once you reach the rail, you ask your horse to push from his hind legs instead of allowing them to trail behind. It also gives riders a way to school the leg-yield with clear aids by checking the impulse to activate the horse until the leg-yield is finished, so he is only receiving one set of aids at once.

Helpful Hints

★ Do not be abrupt with your aids. Look for just a slight acceleration.

★ Maintain light rein contact when you accelerate forward, so you are teaching your horse how to push his body actively forward in good posture, rather than sticking his nose out and falling on the forehand.

1 Begin at **C** in a working walk or jog.

2 At **A**, turn right and proceed up the centerline.

3 When your horse has completed the turn onto the centerline, leg-yield to the rail.

4 When you get to the rail, accelerate forward for a few steps.

5 Repeat the pattern in the opposite direction.

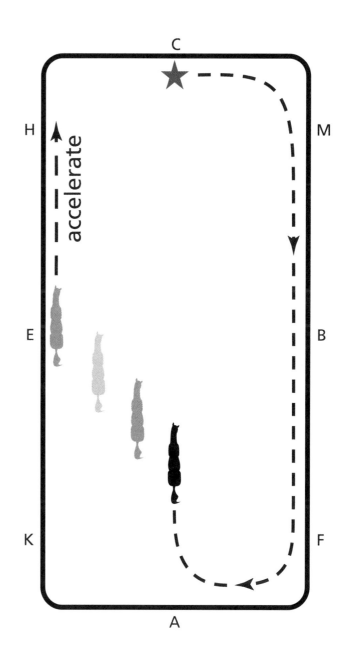

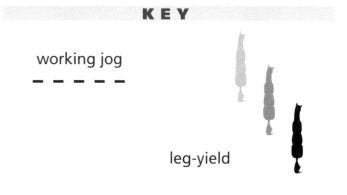

KEY

working jog

- - - - -

leg-yield

53. Working to Lengthened Jog

LEVEL: **BEGINNER**

BENEFITS

This exercise, with its variations in pace, improves collection and encourages swing in the back, while preventing stiffness and dull gaits. The variations help the horse's hind legs move energetically with the activity for collection. Changing pace also keeps the horse "forward-thinking," which means lively but controlled.

Helpful Hints

★ Be sure your horse moves immediately off your leg into a lengthened jog.

★ At the lengthened jog, allow him to stretch his neck longer and lower. The horse should lengthen his frame in addition to his stride.

1 Begin at **A** in a sitting jog.

2 At **F**, ask for a brisk lengthened jog (posting).

3 Proceed posting three-quarters of the way down the long side of the arena.

4 Before **M**, ride a 15-meter circle in a working jog (sitting).

5 Repeat the pattern in the opposite direction.

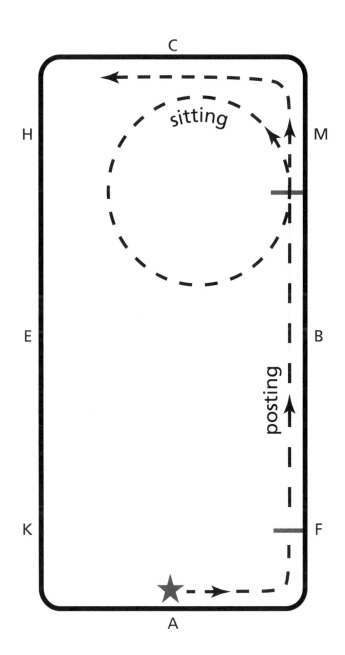

KEY

working jog (sitting)

- - - - - - - -

lengthened jog (posting)

— — — — —

transition

—

54. Two Poles plus a Stride

LEVEL: INTERMEDIATE

BENEFITS

Practicing this exercise delivers unexpected feedback about your effectiveness as a rider. For instance, you might think you are using your seat clearly but then find yourself plowing through the pattern without acing the correct stride counts. Or you might be holding your breath and tightening your hands, which causes your horse to raise his neck and hollow his back.

Exercises like this give tangible, real-time opportunities to realize our tendencies as riders and also give us a chance to fix them. As you can see, all kinds of productive — and fun — work can be accomplished with stride adjustment exercises.

Helpful Hints

★ Try to let your horse adjust his stride between the poles on his own. Sit quietly and do very little.

★ Remember that ground poles are not jumps. The horse should take a normal, lofty lope stride over and between each pole.

1 Set up two poles spaced approximately 16 feet apart, so that your horse can lope one stride after his landing stride before crossing the second pole.

2 Develop a working lope. Be sure you have a relaxed three-beat tempo.

3 Ride over the first pole, take a lope stride, then cross the other pole.

4 Repeat the pattern in both directions.

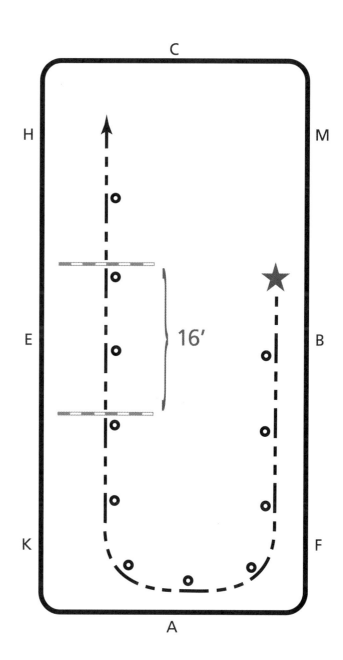

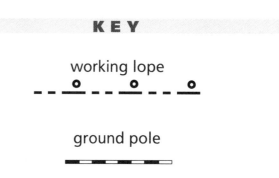

KEY

working lope

ground pole

55. Step Under

LEVEL: BEGINNER

BENEFITS

Diligent practice adjusting the horse's posture, combined with the gentle spinal muscular pulsations from walking, is crucial for maintaining use of the horse's hindquarters. This exercise helps the horse develop good habits for keeping his hind legs engaged. The more he halts with his hind legs well underneath him, the more he will keep them underneath at other times as well.

Helpful Hint

★ Your horse must continue to arch his neck forward and out from his body during the halt, as if actively stretching forward while standing still. Think of him "looking through the bridle." If you lose that stretching attitude of the neck, go back to your walk for a moment, then return to halt. Eventually, you will have the ability to walk his hind feet up toward his front while at the halt.

1 From a marching working walk, ride your horse to a halt, remaining round and on the bit.

2 Maintain contact with his mouth and hold your position: upper body stretched tall, legs resting against your horse's side, elbows bent at your sides, bracing with your back, telling him, "Whoa."

3 Isolate your right lower leg and press it gently against your horse's side, just behind the cinch. Ask him to step forward with his right hind leg while keeping his other legs immobile.

4 When he responds with his right hind leg, even if just a few inches, allow him to stand quietly in balance for a moment.

5 If he's understanding, repeat with the left hind leg.

55. Step Under

56. Collected Walk

LEVEL: **INTERMEDIATE**

BENEFITS

When riders school their horses in collected walk, unfortunate side effects commonly include stiff backs, shortened or irregular strides, and ambling. Use this pattern to work on collected walk correctly. The ground rails maintain the purity of the walk footfalls while also helping the horse achieve slow but lively steps.

Helpful Hint

★ Keep your elbows soft and your rein feel light so you do not block your horse's energy and the lifting of his back when crossing the poles.

1 Set up four poles spaced for your horse's collected walk, approximately 2 feet, 6 inches apart and raised 6 inches off the ground.

2 Ride a 20-meter circle at **E** in a collected walk.

3 On the second half of the circle, ride over the poles. Maintain the same cadence over the poles as when approaching the poles.

4 If your horse knocks the poles, pulls at the reins, or rushes, ask for a halt before proceeding over the poles.

5 Repeat the pattern in the opposite direction.

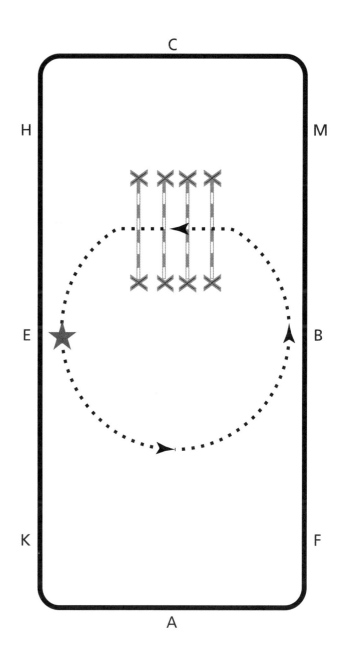

KEY

collected walk
· · · · · · · · · · · · · · ·

ground pole
✗━ ━ ━✗

57. Collect – Extend

LEVEL: **INTERMEDIATE**

BENEFITS

One of the simplest ways to develop extension, this exercise shows the horse how to flow freely out of the collection established by shoulder-in. It gives the rider an important feel of "allowing" extension to happen, rather than pushing it out of the horse.

Helpful Hints

★ For shoulder-in, weight your inside seat bone and keep your inside leg close to the girth. Your outside leg should be positioned slightly behind the girth.

★ Maintain the rhythm of your gait.

★ Visualize lofty strides.

1 Begin at **A** in a collected sitting jog, tracking right.

2 At **K**, develop shoulder-in.

3 Before **E**, turn across the short diagonal.

4 On the short diagonal, ask for an active posting jog.

5 At **M**, resume a sitting jog.

6 Repeat the pattern in the new direction.

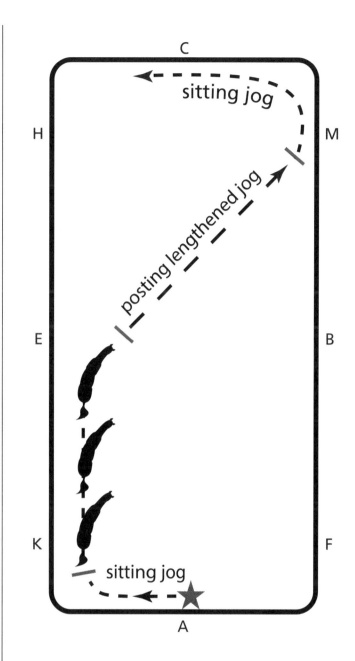

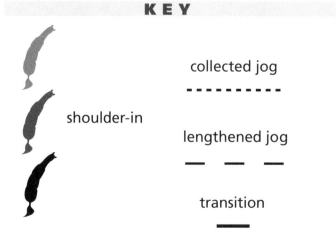

KEY

shoulder-in

collected jog

- - - - - - - - - -

lengthened jog

— — —

transition

—

58. Schaukel #1

LEVEL: **INTERMEDIATE**

In developing any equine athlete, a rider continually needs to think about where the hind legs are. First of all, this demands riding in the correct tempo to build strength. When your horse jogs, watch the motion of his hind legs. Are they swinging forward and landing under his belly or trailing out behind him and landing behind his hip line? If you observe the latter, this indicates poor stifle flexion, and you should increase your tempo during schooling sessions to activate these joints.

The same rule applies to loping, which is why trainers caution riders not to slow the lope tempo before a horse is ready. Without adequate flexion of the joints to draw his hind legs under his belly, it becomes nearly impossible to strengthen his hindquarters.

Once you are riding in the correct tempo for good use of the hind joints, you want to choose exercises that increase strength in the horse's hip flexors, biceps, and quads. Schaukel is an advanced exercise that requires the horse to move from rein-back immediately into a forward gait. As with any gymnastic exercise, use an interval format for this exercise. Ride it in short doses followed by rest periods of equal duration.

Helpful Hints

★ When done well, this should feel like the horse is rocking back and forth smoothly.

★ If your horse throws his head up or braces, get him softer and more responsive before continuing. To do this, ride dozens of walk–halt transitions.

1 At **K**, proceed in a working walk for five steps.

2 Come to a balanced halt.

3 Rein-back four steps.

4 Immediately walk forward again.

5 Repeat this sequence as you ride around the track.

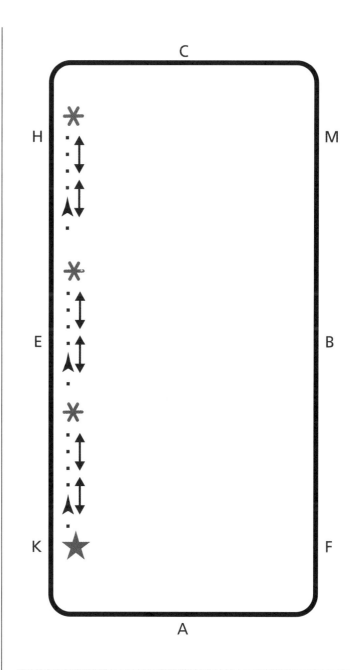

KEY

working walk
· · · · · · · ·

rein-back
↔ ↔

halt ✳

59. Schaukel #2

LEVEL: INTERMEDIATE

BENEFITS

In developing any equine athlete, a rider continually needs to think about where the hind legs are. First of all, this demands riding in the correct tempo to build strength. When your horse jogs, watch the motion of his hind legs. Are they swinging forward and landing under his belly or trailing out behind him and landing behind his hip line? If you observe the latter, this indicates poor stifle flexion, and you should increase your tempo during schooling sessions to activate these joints.

The same rule applies to loping, which is why trainers caution riders not to slow the lope tempo before a horse is ready. Without adequate flexion of the joints to draw his hind legs under his belly, it becomes nearly impossible to strengthen his hindquarters.

Once you are riding in the correct tempo for good use of the hind joints, you want to choose exercises that increase strength in the horse's hip flexors, biceps, and quads. Schaukel is an advanced exercise that requires the horse to move from rein-back immediately into a forward gait. As with any gymnastic exercise, use an interval format for this exercise. Ride it in short doses followed by rest periods of equal duration.

Helpful Hints

★ This is a challenging exercise. Take your time with each step so you don't cue your horse abruptly.

★ If your horse tenses up after the rein-back, allow him one or two steps of walk when transitioning back to jog.

★ Smoothness and balance are more important than quickness.

1 At **K**, proceed in a working jog for several steps.

2 Halt immobile for 3 seconds.

3 Rein-back four steps.

4 Immediately proceed again in a working jog.

5 Repeat this sequence as you ride around the arena.

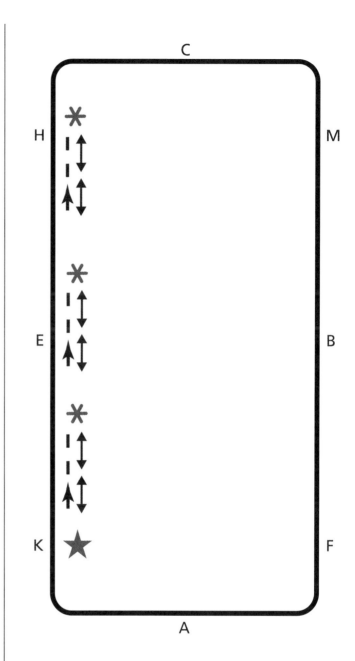

KEY

working jog

– – – – –

rein-back

↔ ↔

halt ✳

60. Collection Serpentines

LEVEL: INTERMEDIATE

BENEFITS

The serpentine is an excellent exercise for symmetry in the horse's musculoskeletal system and also for rider accuracy. This exercise is especially useful when a horse likes to bulge out with one shoulder or when a rider has a weaker leg. Patterns like this are effective for developing engagement in lethargic or lazy horses because the long, straight lines help send the horse's energy forward.

Helpful Hints

★ Geometry is important here. Make sure each loop is the same size.

★ Begin to collect and bend well ahead of each turn. Prepare a few strides before you come to the turn.

1 At a jog, ride a three-loop serpentine, using the length of the arena for each loop.

2 On each arc, collect the jog.

3 As you come out of the arc and head straight, lengthen the strides down the arena.

4 At the next arc, collect again.

5 Make clear distinctions between your collections and lengthenings.

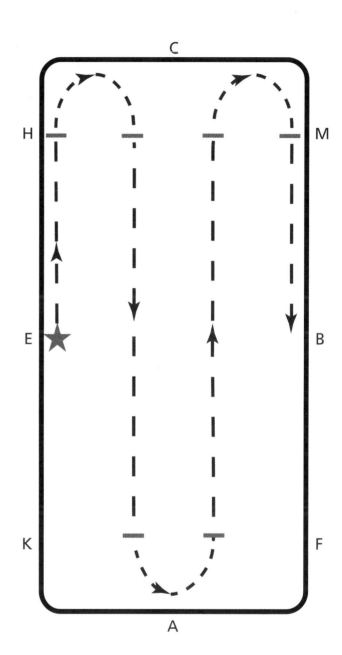

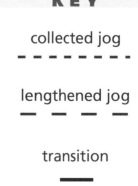

KEY

collected jog
- - - - - - -

lengthened jog
– – – –

transition
▬▬▬

61. Jog Half-pass

LEVEL: **INTERMEDIATE**

BENEFITS

Using the magnetic pull of the rail, this exercise helps teach half-pass by giving the horse a clear sense of direction. This helps maintain energy and impulsion in the movement.

Helpful Hints

★ Your half-pass should flow smoothly from a well-ridden circle. If the 12-meter circle falls apart (your horse loses rhythm, bend, or contact), do not attempt the half-pass.

★ If your horse frequently gets stuck or loses tempo on the half-pass, it sometimes helps to ride it while posting, rather than sitting.

1 Begin at **B** in a working jog, tracking left.

2 In the corner between **M** and **C** ride a 12-meter circle.

3 Ride halfway around the circle again.

4 Half-pass back to the rail at **B**.

5 Repeat this pattern in both directions.

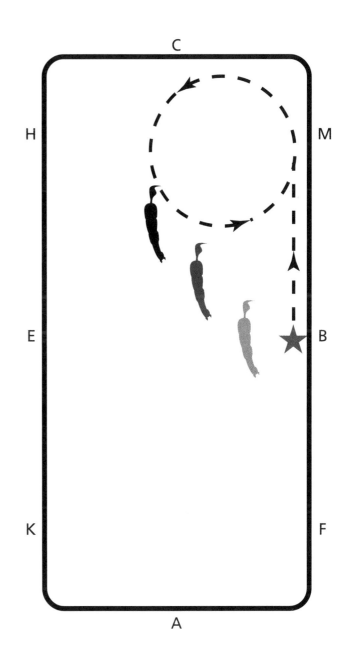

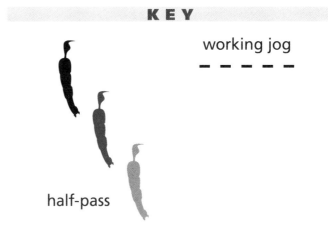

KEY

working jog

- - - - -

half-pass

62. Lope Bowtie

LEVEL: **INTERMEDIATE**

BENEFITS

A horse that uses both sides of his body equally is like a piece of warm metal — bendable and unrestricted. By practicing short bouts of lope on each lead, interspersed with the rebalancing of downward and upward transitions, this exercise asks the horse to keep reorganizing his body. This in turn makes him more efficient, confident, and engaged in each direction.

Helpful Hint

★ When making the lope-jog-lope transition, act like you have all the time in the world. Too many riders rush these strides, and then things fall apart. It's better to be a little late than abrupt.

1 Begin in a lope, left lead.

2 In the corner at **M** ride a 12-meter half-circle.

3 Just before returning to the rail at **B**, transition to a jog.

4 Proceed past **B** for four to five strides in a jog. Organize as needed.

5 Pick up a lope, right lead.

6 In the next corner at **F**, ride a 12-meter half-circle.

7 Just before returning to the track at **B**, transition to a jog.

8 Repeat the sequence.

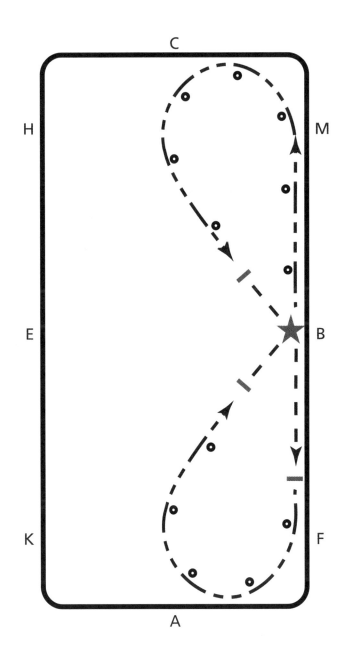

KEY

working jog
– – – – – – –

transition
––––

working lope
– – ○ – – ○ – –

63. Counter to True

LEVEL: **INTERMEDIATE**

BENEFITS

Counter-lope tones the same region of the horse's body as haunches-in and half-pass, requiring quite a bit of stability through the lower back and hips. When a horse is not adequately prepared, it can make him sore. Counter-lope is best practiced with patterns like this that ask for it in short segments, with the ability to refresh the horse's energy and looseness with true lope as needed.

Helpful Hints

★ The 15-meter circle in true lope can be used to refresh the horse's energy if he is beginning to struggle or falter in the counter-lope.

★ Energize him on that circle and be sure to bend him well to the right. Then maintain that bend and energy in your counter-lope.

1 At the end of the arena near **F**, pick up a counter-lope, right lead.

2 Halfway to **B**, begin a 20-meter circle in a counter-lope.

3 At the centerline, make a 15-meter circle to the right, maintaining the right lead (in true lope).

4 Proceed in a counter-lope around the 20-meter circle.

5 If your horse begins to falter in the counter-lope, ride another 15-meter circle to the right in a true lope at the next centerline.

6 Repeat the pattern in the opposite direction.

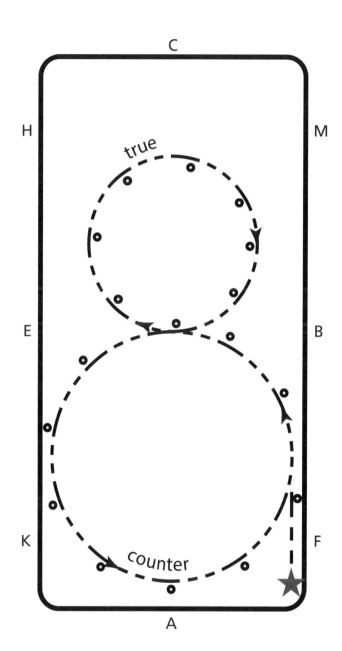

KEY

working lope

counter-lope

64. Counter-lope Serpentine

LEVEL: INTERMEDIATE

BENEFITS

Simple in shape but less so in execution, shallow serpentines are quite sophisticated in terms of how they test and what they offer the horse. To perform them accurately, a horse must be balanced and symmetrical enough to maintain his rhythm exactly, keep his topline rounded, and establish correct soft lateral flexion. Shallow serpentines are often preferable over more complicated figures with steeper turns or multiple arcs because they preserve the horse's forward energy and therefore keep his hind legs under his body.

Often they are the simplest way to create more symmetry or suppleness, and the simplest training techniques are generally the best. Especially when a horse needs to overcome crookedness or stiffness, shallow serpentines are a fluid way to increase symmetry because they don't require direction changes. The goal is accomplished by alternating which of his hind legs is bearing more weight and by bending his spine back and forth.

Helpful Hints

★ Reminders for counter-lope aids:

- Weight the stirrup and seat bone on the side of your horse's leading leg.
- Maintain lateral flexion in the direction of your horse's leading leg.
- Support the movement with your outside leg against your horse, positioned behind the cinch.
- Sit still and navigate clearly.

1 Ride a three-loop serpentine from C in a working lope, right lead.

2 Maintain the right lead throughout the entire serpentine.

3 On the middle loop, ride counter-lope by maintaining your horse's right bend and keeping his tempo steady.

4 If your horse struggles or braces, try starting with the modified shallow loop shown.

5 Repeat the pattern in the opposite direction, maintaining the left lead throughout.

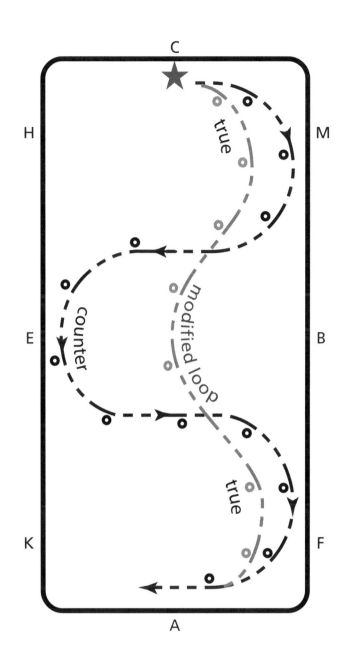

KEY

working lope

counter-lope

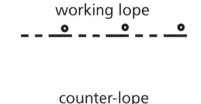

65. Lope Half-pass #1

LEVEL: **ADVANCED**

BENEFITS

Unparalleled in their ability to lighten the forehand and supple the horse's shoulders, half-passes are one of the achievements of strong foundational training. When introducing them at a lope, it is best to practice small segments so that the horse does not have time to fall apart or struggle for balance. Developing good lope half-passes will prepare the horse for clean flying changes and more advanced work such as lope pirouettes.

Helpful Hints

★ If your horse gets stuck in the sideways movement, go back and refresh lope leg-yields.

★ In half-pass, be sure that your horse clearly looks and flexes toward where he is heading.

1 Track left in a collected lope starting at **A**.

2 Ride a deep corner between **M** and **C**, developing a clear left bend.

3 Past **C**, turn left on the quarter line, maintaining the left bend.

4 Weight your left seat bone, apply your right leg, and half-pass to the rail between **B** and **F**.

5 At the rail, transition to jog or walk.

6 Repeat the pattern in the opposite direction on the right lead.

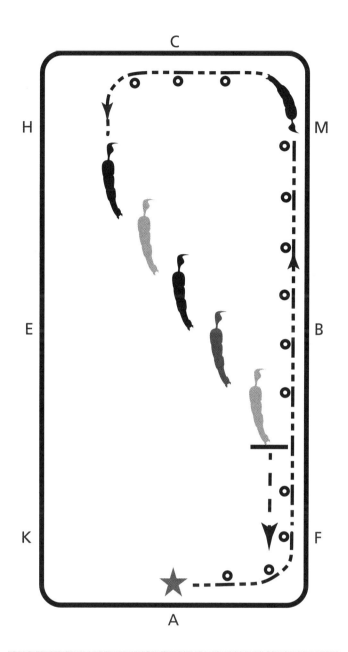

KEY

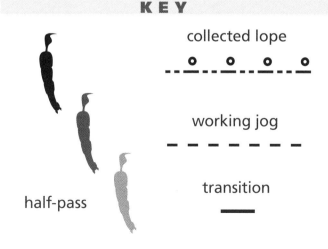

collected lope

working jog

transition

half-pass

66. Lope Half-pass #2

LEVEL: ADVANCED

BENEFITS

Unparalleled in their ability to lighten the forehand and supple the horse's shoulders, half-passes are one of the achievements of strong foundational training. When introducing them at a lope, it is best to practice small segments so that the horse does not have time to fall apart or struggle for balance. Developing good lope half-passes will prepare the horse for clean flying changes and more advanced work such as lope pirouettes.

Helpful Hints

★ This exercise nicely follows exercises of turns on the haunches.

★ In this pattern, we ask the horse to mobilize his shoulders first with shoulder-in, then begin the half-pass.

★ Be sure to maintain a three-beat lope in the half-pass. If you begin losing the rhythm, return to a working lope.

1 Ride a 15-meter circle at **A** in collected lope to warm up your bend.

2 Continue straight, and at **K** ask for a stride of shoulder-in.

3 Half-pass to **X**.

4 Proceed straight ahead at **X**, maintaining a collected lope.

5 Repeat the pattern in the opposite direction.

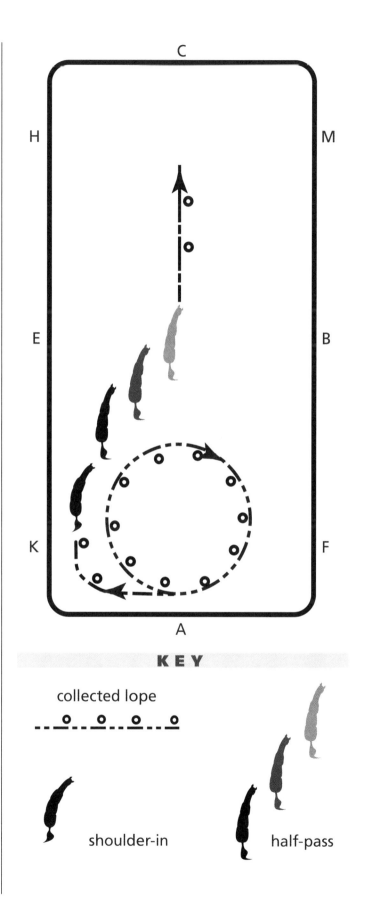

KEY

collected lope

shoulder-in

half-pass

67. Pirouette to Half-pass

LEVEL: **ADVANCED**

BENEFITS

This exercise threads together lateral movements to build strength in the horse's hindquarters by having him maintain lateral flexion while reorganizing his legs. To do this without falling out of balance, he needs to recruit his deep underlying postural muscles. This is the stepping stone to more complex and advanced graceful movements in dressage.

Helpful Hints

★ Keep your horse looking in the direction of your bend.

★ Your horse needs a clear sense of direction and travel to prevent planting his hind feet.

★ You want him to remain active, with the feeling that he could jog at any moment.

1 Begin at **A** in a working walk.

2 Turn left up the quarter line. Walk straight forward several strides.

3 Collect the strides and ride a half-pirouette to the left.

4 On the final step of your half-pirouette, maintain the left bend.

5 Then immediately proceed in half-pass left to the rail at **F**.

6 Execute in both directions.

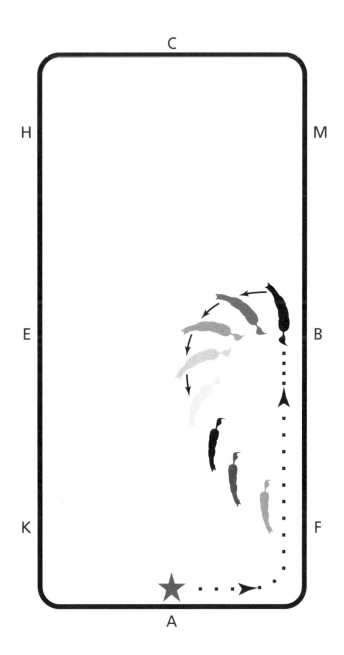

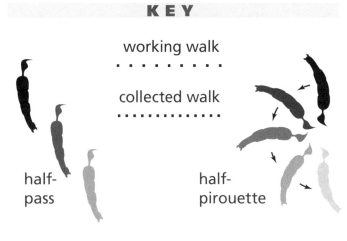

KEY

working walk

· · · · · · · · · ·

collected walk

· · · · · · · · · ·

half-pass

half-pirouette

68. Very Collected Strides

LEVEL: **ADVANCED**

BENEFITS

The ability to lope with rhythmic and relaxed foot-falls is one of the primary goals for the gait. Of equal importance, however, is the balance and looseness necessary to maintain a slow lofty lope while also maintaining utmost softness in the horse's neck. Too often, horses lope around with stiff, braced-up necks, the result of learning to balance themselves by restricting the musculature that controls the oscillations throughout their spines.

The neck muscling, even when arched in a frame for dressage, should show relaxation and allow the natural movement of the horse's head and neck forward and backward with each stride, the same as in the walk. Horses that lope with their necks held in static, fixed postures are doing a disservice to the rest of their spinal joints and consequently the lumbar-sacral region, which dictates the movement of their hind limbs.

Helpful Hints

★ Be sure that the size and shape of your figure does not change when transitioning to and from collection. Many riders tend to collapse the circle.

★ Aim to make a very clear distinction between your working and collected lope. Imagine that anyone watching you should be able to see the distinction.

1 Ride a 20-meter circle at **A** in working lope, right lead.

2 As you cross over the quarter line, collect the lope.

3 Ride in a highly collected lope for four to five strides, crossing over the centerline.

4 Allow your horse to resume a working lope at the next quarter line.

5 Continue the pattern.

6 Practice equally in both directions.

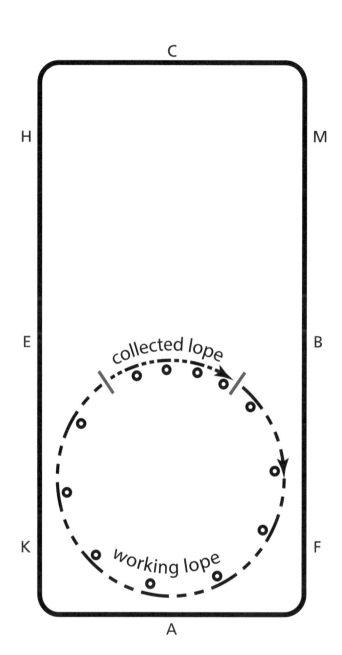

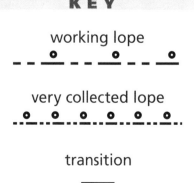

KEY

working lope

very collected lope

transition

69. Shoulder-in on Circle

LEVEL: ADVANCED

BENEFITS

Many horses learn shoulder-in more easily on a circle where they are able to adopt the positioning from an already curved body posture. This exercise is the answer for horses that become evasive (swinging hindquarters around, hollowing topline, and so on) when learning shoulder-in on straight lines. It also builds strength in the horse's quadriceps, and gluteus muscles and the many small muscles in the chest floor.

Helpful Hints

★ Think about bringing your horse's front legs onto a smaller circle while his back feet remain on the 20-meter circle.

★ Sit up tall and use your outside leg to turn your horse's shoulders for shoulder-in steps.

★ Practice in walk, if needed.

1 Ride a 20-meter circle at **B**, tracking left in a working jog.

2 On one side of the circle, rotate yourself and your horse's front end toward the middle of the circle.

3 Ride a few steps in shoulder-in.

4 Straighten to resume riding around the 20-meter circle.

5 Repeat the pattern several times.

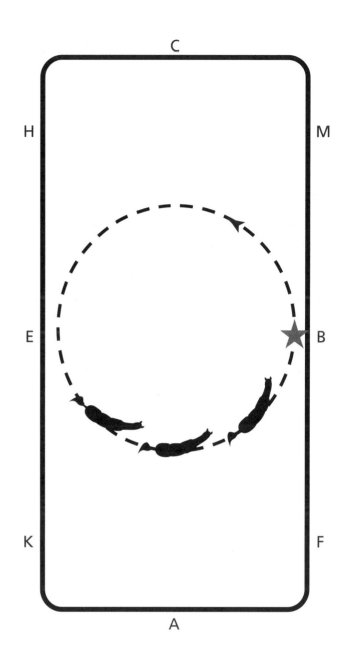

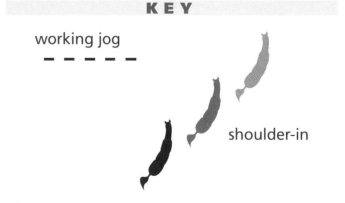

KEY

working jog

– – – – –

shoulder-in

70. Counter-lope Circle 8s

LEVEL: **ADVANCED**

BENEFITS

Once confirmed in a decent collected lope, all horses should develop counter-lope. It has a primary gymnastic effect of creating a straighter-moving horse. It also challenges the horse's balance, thereby developing greater collection in the lope. A rider must become very proficient at exercises like this one before being able to ride flying changes and complex lope patterns.

Helpful Hints

★ Be sure to master the introductory counter-lope exercises (Exercises 63 and 64) before tackling this one.

★ In the counter-lope, your horse should become more collected but continue thinking "forward."

1 At **A**, develop a working lope, left lead.

2 Ride a 20-meter circle.

3 Ride halfway around the circle again.

4 At the centerline, leave that circle and begin a 20-meter circle to the right.

5 Maintain the left lead for a counter-lope around the new circle.

6 When you reach the centerline again, return to and complete your original circle to the left.

7 Repeat the pattern in the opposite direction, maintaining the right lead.

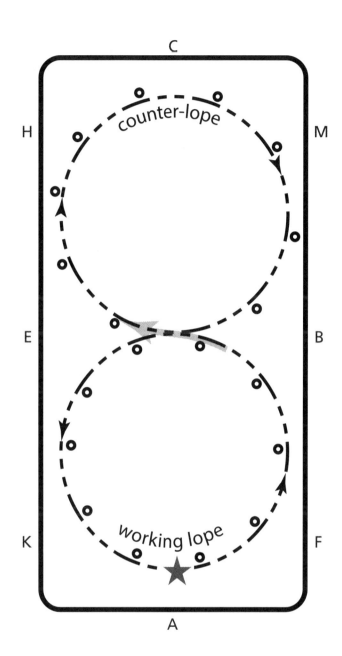

KEY

working lope

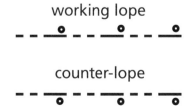

counter-lope

71. Rein-back to Lope

LEVEL: **ADVANCED**

BENEFITS

This exercise follows after much practice with Schaukel exercises (see Exercises 58 and 59). It is suited for mature and well-conditioned horses, not youngsters or those out of shape. This footwork helps the horse develop more engagement in both upward and downward transitions. Also, the rein-back stretches the horse's hamstrings, which is always a welcome gymnastic effect when collection is required.

Helpful Hints

★ If your walk-to-lope transitions are not smooth and perfectly straight, you are not ready for this exercise.

★ If your horse executes this exercise by repeatedly lifting his head and neck and lurching into the lope, return to transitions just between walk and lope to reconnect him over his topline.

★ Be sure to sit tall and quiet. Many riders make the mistake of trying to "shove" the horse forward with their upper bodies.

1 After a thorough warm-up, ask your horse to halt while remaining on the bit.

2 Ask your horse to rein-back six steps.

3 Maintain a light feel of his mouth.

4 After the final step back, ask him to depart immediately in a lope.

5 Repeat the exercise 3 times on each lead.

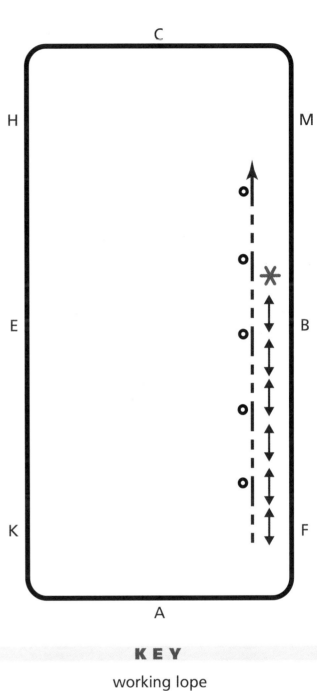

KEY

working lope

rein-back

halt ✳

72. Lope Pirouette

LEVEL: **ADVANCED**

Suitable only for advanced horses and riders, the pirouette is the crowning achievement of collection in the lope. It is the utmost test of strength and balance and harmony with the rider's aids. Never practice more than a few pirouettes in a week, as the exercise can tax the horse's hocks.

Helpful Hints

★ Prepare your horse for this exercise with some working pirouettes at a walk to be sure you are coordinating your aids the same way.

★ If your preparation steps at K don't go well (horse braces, loses the lope, or speeds up) practice more steps like these, including on circles, until they are very smooth. Then come back to try the pirouette.

1 At **A**, track right in a collected lope.

2 At **K**, ask your horse to bring his haunches slightly inside for two strides.

3 Make sure his response is soft and immediate and his lope stays rhythmic.

4 Proceed straight in a collected lope.

5 Just before the corner at **H**, again ask him to bring his haunches slightly to the inside.

6 Keeping your outside leg back, ask him to move his front end around his back end.

7 Imagine his whole body rotating around his right hind foot.

8 Repeat the exercise in the opposite direction on the left lead.

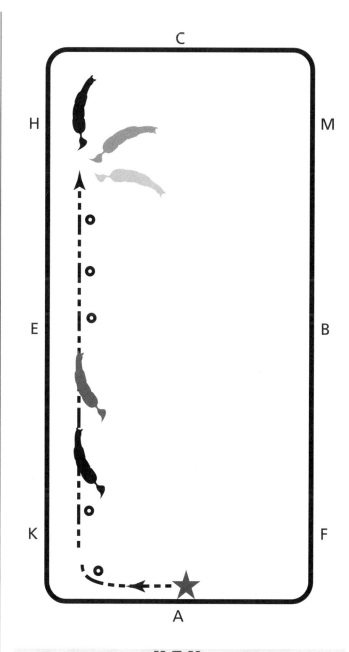

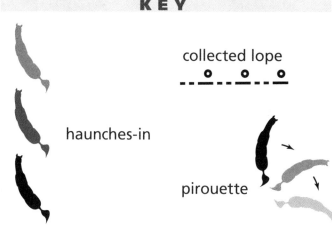

KEY

collected lope

haunches-in

pirouette

CHAPTER 6

ADJUSTABILITY

RIDING CIRCLES is a time-honored exercise, but too often, after revolving around and around, riders forget why or how they ended up on a circle in the first place. Same goes for meandering through serpentines and squares. Was this figure supposed to bend the horse? Or was it for another purpose altogether?

Admittedly, it's easy to be a victim of random circles or absentminded loops and turns. To the uninitiated, arena figures might seem like a grab bag where riders cruise through whichever shapes pop into their heads. However, arena figures exist for specific purposes, not the least of which is to help the horse organize his body.

In dressage we use the progressive advancement of figures to improve a horse's balance, straightness, and strength. We use different shapes — circle, half-turn, square, and so on — at particular times to ask the horse to organize his body. If you keep this in mind, you begin to see how arena patterns are themselves aids and why certain ones are suitable at particular times in a horse's development, while others are not.

Just like half-halts, seat and leg cues, or rein aids, arena figures serve the purpose of changing the horse's equilibrium, activating his hindquarters, and loosening his back, among other postural changes. The trick is to know which figure to ride in any given workout. Effective clinicians often help illuminate which exercises will benefit a horse at its particular stage of training. Learning to choose from your toolbox of patterns is one secret to becoming a successful rider, rather than just riding around aimlessly.

To simplify things when learning dressage, think of the influence that any available figure might have on these three areas with your horse: adjusting his speed, organizing his spine, or developing symmetry in his body. When you ride any shape, ask yourself if and how it targets one of these areas. Notice, for example, that riding a circle helps your young horse's rushing jog slow down and become more balanced. As soon as he organizes himself by adjusting his speed, it's time to leave the circle rather than repeating it to the point of dulling or losing what you just accomplished. In this way the circle joins your seat, voice, and reins as an aid to help the horse perform better.

The same concept applies for youngsters on a shallow serpentine or loop. Ridden with purpose, these arcs ask the horse to switch his inside weight-bearing leg and to change direction of his spinal flexion, all without losing his rhythm or altering his longitudinal balance. In other words, they develop symmetry between both sides of his body. Some riders may have been riding shallow serpentines for months without realizing what it is they are actually asking the horse to accomplish.

As a general rule, tighter turns such as squares and multiple quick changes of direction require more collection and advanced balance from the horse, so they are saved for higher levels of training. If you find yourself unclear, though, about *why* an instructor might be telling you to ride a particular figure, don't be afraid to ask. It is perfectly acceptable to say: "Remind me what this figure accomplishes for my horse."

This way, training and riding — especially taking instruction — will seem much less like a random set of directives. It will make you a more effective rider to understand how to use figures as an additional set of aids, rather than resorting to exaggerated seat or rein cues. Remember that the shapes and patterns we ride have evolved over a long period of history. There is indeed logic behind them.

73. Flat Top

LEVEL: **BEGINNER**

BENEFITS

Keeping the horse properly bent and balanced between the rider's inside and outside legs is always trickier than it seems like it should be, but the inability to do it accounts for many riders' lopsided circles. Accurately ridden figures are your best training tools, which is why exercises like this one get such big results. This pattern cleans up any tendency to ride misshapen circles. It also improves the horse's responsiveness.

Helpful Hints

★ Most riders think they are riding a straight line when they are actually riding an arc in the lope. Set up cones to be sure!

★ Keep your outside leg against the horse to maintain a good straight line.

1 Set up four cones as shown, to form a pair of "gates."

2 Beginning at **E**, ride a 20-meter circle in working lope, left lead.

3 After passing **B**, ride straight across the arena, through the gates.

4 When you reach the opposite rail, return to your circle.

5 Repeat the pattern in the opposite direction on the right lead.

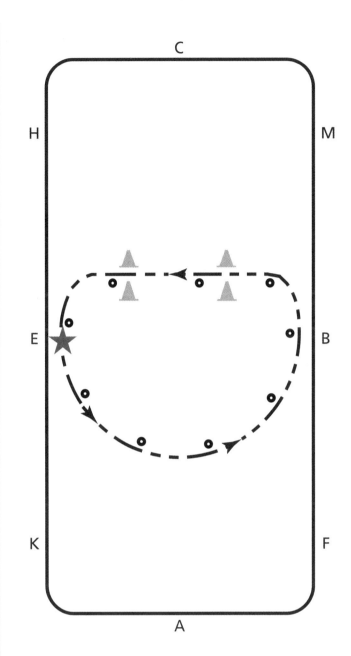

K E Y

working lope

cone

74. Serpentine through Lanes

LEVEL: **BEGINNER**

BENEFITS

Riding through chutes helps the rider create better balance on bending lines by preventing the tendency to lean inward on a turn or collapse over the inside hip, which then causes too much inside rein pressure and other imbalances. This exercise keeps the rider sitting squarely while riding effective bending aids.

Helpful Hints

★ Be sure to enter and exit the ground-pole lanes in the exact center.

★ Count your strides through the ground-pole chute and aim for the same number of strides in each chute.

1 Set up two pairs of 8-foot poles to form two channels each 4 feet apart, as shown.

2 Begin at a working jog at C.

3 Ride a three-loop serpentine, passing through the center of each channel.

4 At A, repeat the serpentine.

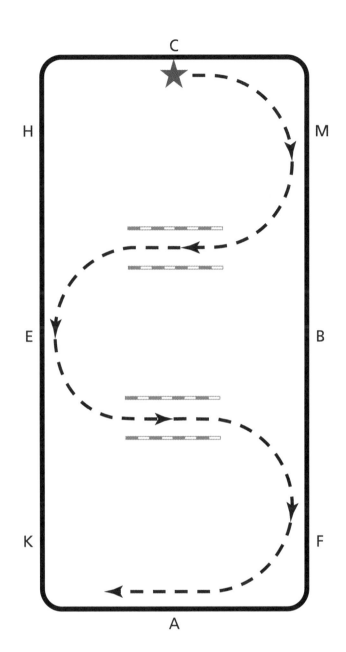

KEY

working jog

– – – – –

ground pole

75. Diamond-shaped Circle

LEVEL: INTERMEDIATE

BENEFITS

Especially useful for riders or horses with a dominant side, this exercise fixes wobbly or collapsed circles. It is tremendously useful when horses or riders fall in toward the middle of the circle. When a horse struggles to bend in a particular direction due to stiffness or lack of balance, this exercise can remedy the problem. Further, it makes riders balance more effectively on every stride rather than just being a passenger. By bringing accurate geometry to otherwise disorganized circles, it prevents the horse from traveling around in a compromised posture.

Helpful Hints

★ Do not make the common mistake of rotating your upper body in an exaggerated way. Think of turning your shoulders *with* your horse's shoulders.

★ Be sure to keep even tension in both reins. If you take up too much weight on one rein or another, your horse's neck will not remain straight, causing your figure to be wobbly.

★ The key to this exercise is using your outside turning leg effectively without getting twisted in your seat and upper body.

★ This pattern improves how you ride circles by tuning you in to where your horse's feet are. You may initially find it necessary to slow down upon approaching each cone, so you and your horse have a chance to gather yourselves for a good sharp turn.

1 Set up four cones as shown to make a diamond shape within a 20-meter circle.

2 At **E** track right in walk or jog. Square your hips toward the cone sitting on the centerline.

3 Just before the cone, turn your body and focus on the next cone.

4 While making the turn to the next cone, sit heavier on your inside seat bone and close your outside leg more against your horse.

5 Envision riding a perfect 90-degree turn at each cone.

6 Be sure your diamond feels smooth and even in both a walk and jog in each direction.

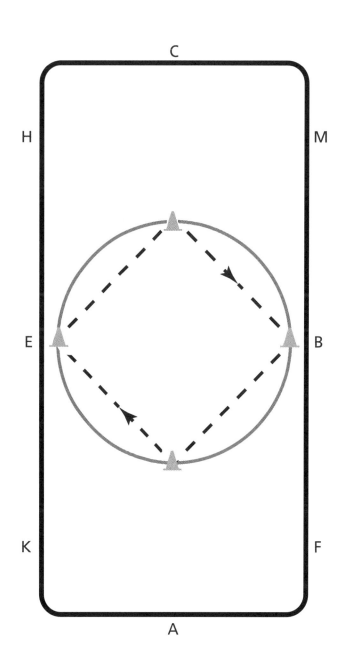

KEY

working jog

– – – – –

cone ▲

76. Octagon-shaped Circle

LEVEL: **INTERMEDIATE**

BENEFITS

Like the previous exercise, this one helps riders or horses with a dominant side fix wobbly or collapsed circles, particularly when either one has a tendency to fall in toward the middle of the circle. When a horse struggles to bend in a particular direction because of stiffness or lack of balance, this exercise can remedy the problem. Further, it makes riders balance more effectively on every stride rather than just being a passenger. By bringing accurate geometry to otherwise disorganized circles, it prevents the horse from traveling around in a compromised posture.

Helpful Hints

★ If you are not reaching your points exactly, check your speed. Fluctuations in tempo will throw off your line.

★ Make sure your outside rein is steady on these little octagon turns. A good connection on your outside rein helps your horse bring his shoulders around the turn while remaining flexed through his spine.

1 Set up eight cones as shown to make an octagon shape within a 20-meter circle.

2 Begin in a working jog and ride point-to-point around the octagon.

3 One stride before each cone, look ahead to the next cone.

4 Make sure the octagon feels smooth and even in each direction.

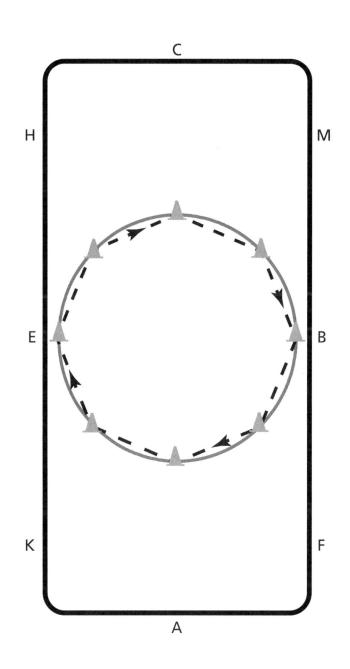

KEY

working jog

— — — — —

cone ▲

77. Figure 8 Lengthening

LEVEL: **INTERMEDIATE**

This pattern is effective because it brings the horse back into balance so quickly — through use of a bend — after the short distance of lengthening strides that he is not able to fall on the forehand or start rushing. Using in our favor the horse's ability to anticipate, a few repetitions of this exercise will result in the horse beginning to lower and engage his hindquarters almost on his own upon reaching the end of the short diagonal.

Helpful Hint

★ Use the bends of the arcs to get the horse as balanced as possible. Then to lengthen, spend a bit more time pushing forward in the air as you rise and a bit less time relaxing down as you sit. This will help "lift" your horse and create suspension in his strides.

1 Ride two 20-meter half-circles connected by short, straight diagonal lines.

2 On the half-circles, ask your horse for a collected jog.

3 As soon as you turn onto the short diagonal to make the figure of 8, begin posting and ask for a lengthened jog stride.

4 After crossing the short diagonal line, resume a collected jog, sitting for the new half-circle.

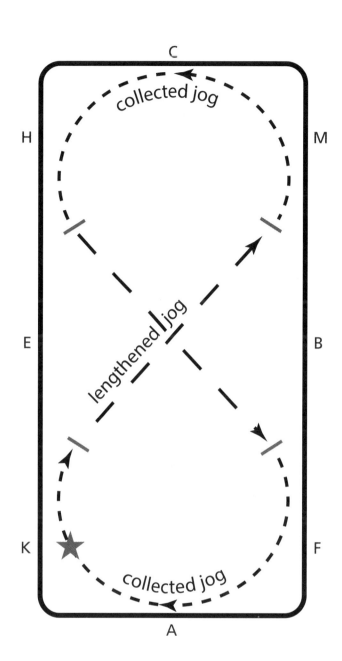

KEY

collected jog

– – – – – – – –

lengthened jog

– – – – –

transition

—

78. Circle – Square

LEVEL: **INTERMEDIATE**

BENEFITS

Hands-down, the most common problem riders encounter is how horses' natural crookedness affects their performance. Especially when carrying a rider, this natural crookedness creates gait deficiencies, weakness, and hindrances to performance.

Well-ridden circles are the best way to help fix a horse's asymmetry, but they bring the risk of leading to compromises. When asked to ride a circle, the crooked horse develops sore muscles, bracing patterns, shorter strides, and stiffness. This exercise improves your horse's symmetry without riding around in endless circles and also requires constant adjustment and skillfulness from the rider.

This is a simple exercise, but do set up cones to be sure that your square is actually square. We tend to fool ourselves otherwise. This exercise can be ridden in all three gaits.

Helpful Hints

★ If your horse has any crookedness, it will show up here. This exercise requires you to ride both the inside and outside of the horse's body.

★ Look up and plan your line.

★ If you tend to cheat on your square corners, ask a ground person to watch you.

1 Set up a cone at each corner of a 20-meter square, as shown.

2 Begin at **A** in a walk or jog. Ride a 20-meter circle.

3 Immediately after, ride a 20-meter square with 90-degree corners.

4 Alternate back and forth between riding a circle and riding a square.

5 Once you've mastered the exercise at a jog, try it at the lope and in both directions.

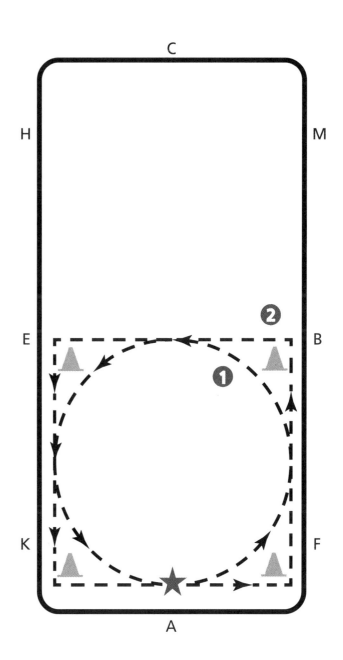

KEY

working jog – – – –

cone ▲

79. Pentagon Turns

LEVEL: **INTERMEDIATE**

BENEFITS

This exercise offers a fluid way of connecting several turns on the haunches. The markers help create direction for both horse and rider, so that the hind legs are kept under the body and marching a purposeful line rather than drifting aimlessly. The forward movement between cones helps keep the horse soft by refreshing his energy before again asking him to pivot around his hind end.

Helpful Hints

★ Take your time at each turn. If your halt is unbalanced, the turn on the haunches will not be successful.

★ Accurate geometry is important. Use your markers!

1 Set up 5 cones or markers in a pentagon shape with 10 meters between each marker.

2 Develop a working walk.

3 At each cone, come to a balanced halt.

4 Turn on the haunches for two to three steps.

5 Proceed straight ahead to the next cone.

6 Repeat the pattern in the opposite direction.

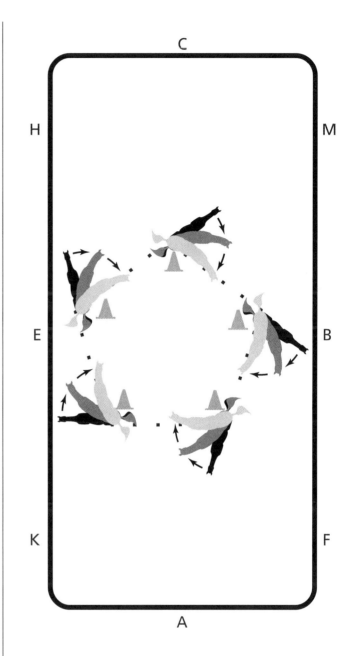

KEY

working walk

cone

turn on haunches

80. Leave One Out

LEVEL: **INTERMEDIATE**

BENEFITS

The adjustments of balance in this pattern mean that your horse will recruit muscles at varying rates of speed and intensity. This prevents him from plodding along with gaits that are stuck in one particular gear. It shakes things up a little, encouraging him to release tension in his back and promote more flexion in the hind legs. The bottom line is that this simple pattern helps the horse use his whole structure better and the ground poles help him develop flexion in the hind joints, a precursor to correct flexion.

Helpful Hint

★ Be sure to ride as if you were crossing a pole. Keep the lift in your chest, and let your hips really swing. Hug your legs close to your horse's sides.

1 Set up six ground poles spaced for your horse's jog stride (3 feet, 6 inches to 4 feet). Remove the fifth pole to leave a blank space.

2 Begin in a working jog and ride over the five remaining poles as if there were actually six poles.

3 When riding over the blank space, imagine your horse lifting his legs over the missing pole and keeping the cadence from the previous four poles all on his own.

4 Ride over the pole formation five times, then take a 30-second break before repeating the exercise.

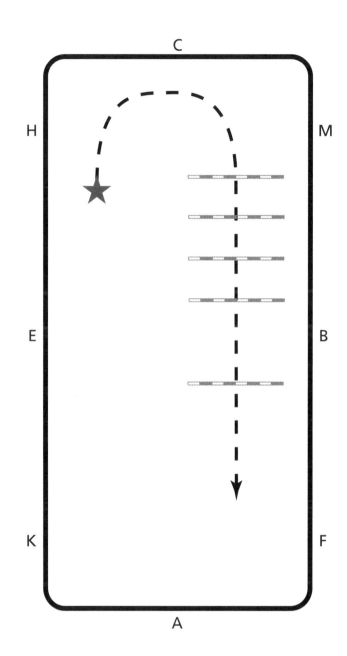

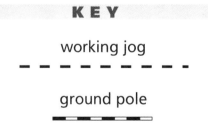

KEY

working jog

– – – – – – –

ground pole

81. Leave One Out, Lope

LEVEL: **INTERMEDIATE**

BENEFITS

When a horse lopes with his hind legs trailing or is stiff or hurrying, he pushes his weight onto his front legs. This extra weight causes him to put his front legs down more quickly to catch his balance on each stride. The rider then loses the feeling of loftiness needed in the lope strides to create collection. In a collected, springy lope, a rider feels the horse's balance going uphill in front of the saddle like riding a carousel horse.

Pole work provides a means of rebalancing a horse that lopes with hurried or choppy strides. Loping over a pole on the ground causes the horse to be more precise with his foot placement during a stride, which means he goes about the stride differently from normal. This interruption in his typically gravity-laden stride allows the rider to show him how to use his body better.

By teaching the horse to travel up to and over the pole with a specific rhythm and preparation, we can help him change his lope mechanics. By altering placement of poles, we can help him put his feet down either more quickly or more slowly. When we gain this adjustability in his stride, we help him use his back and hindquarters more correctly for uphill balance.

Helpful Hint

★ Lope poles develop your horse's lope with more uphill balance and loft. In order to help with this, be sure not to lean forward over poles. They are not jumps. Remain fully seated.

1 Set up four ground poles spaced for lope strides (approximately 8-10 feet apart). Remove the third pole to leave a blank space.

2 Begin in a working lope.

3 Cross the first two poles as a "bounce" (allowing no lope strides between the poles).

4 Then proceed ahead to the final pole, allowing one lope stride between the second and third poles.

5 Execute the pattern 5 times on each lead.

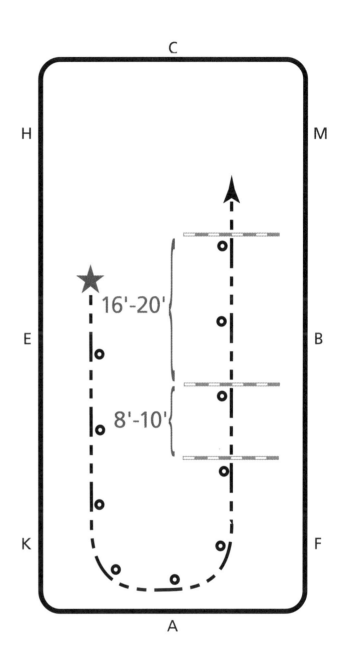

K E Y

working lope

ground pole

82. Lengthen to Leg-yield

LEVEL: INTERMEDIATE

BENEFITS

Although drilling patterns repeatedly is usually not beneficial, it can be helpful to ride this exercise through several times in a row, for two reasons. First, as the horse repeats each leg-yield he becomes looser in his movement and more supple, allowing him to cover more ground in the lengthened jog strides. Second, each of the short diagonals allows you to tune up your horse's responsiveness to moving well forward promptly when asked.

Helpful Hints

★ There are a lot of little cues to organize in this exercise, and the details determine its success. Specifically, focus on how well your horse responds to your half halts.

★ Confirm the exercise in the walk before riding it in the jog.

★ Look and plan ahead to avoid abrupt transitions.

★ Think of flowing from forward to sideways movement.

1 Begin at **A** in a working jog or walk.

2 At **K**, turn on the short diagonal toward **B**.

3 Ask your horse to lengthen his strides.

4 When you reach the quarter line before **B**, turn left up the quarter line and resume your working gait.

5 Immediately leg-yield from the quarter line to the rail, arriving at **M**.

6 Repeat the pattern in the opposite direction.

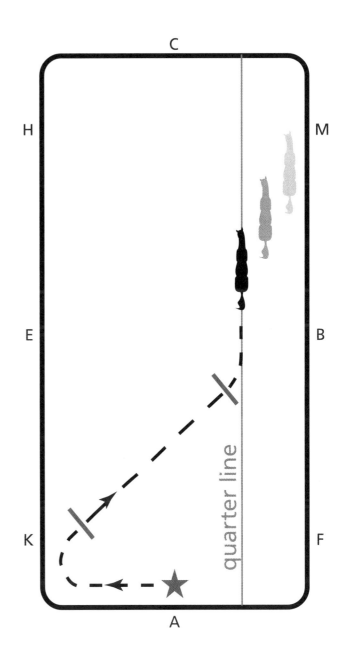

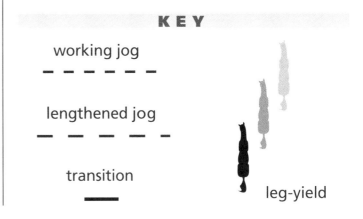

KEY

working jog

lengthened jog

transition

leg-yield

83. Spiral In to Turn on Forehand

LEVEL: **INTERMEDIATE**

BENEFITS

Developing the beginnings of a maneuverable horse, this exercise is sometimes referred to as a *giravolta* in classical texts. It helps the horse gain all the positive benefits of lateral suppling while assisting the rider in controlling alignment and footwork. In particular, it gives consistent practice executing lateral steps by first initiating proper inside flexion at the poll.

This exercise is often highly successful with horses that have learned to brace their necks or pull on the reins when asked to yield away from the rider's leg. It helps the rider preserve softness each step along the way.

Helpful Hints

★ Take your time to achieve lateral flexion fully each time through. Ensure this degree of flexion is equal as you repeat the exercise in each direction.

★ Most horses have one direction where you will find the flexion trickier to establish. Continue to ask yourself, "Can I see his inside eye?" Any time the answer is no, cease the pattern briefly and reestablish lateral flexion before carrying on.

★ This pattern is best executed when followed by energetic forward riding to refresh the horse's energy.

1 Develop a working walk on a 20-meter circle to the left.

2 Begin to spiral inward, reducing your circle size approximately 3 meters on each revolution of the circle.

3 When you get down to a tiny circle and cannot shrink it any further, stop your horse's front feet.

4 Establish left flexion so you can clearly see the horse's left eye.

5 Immediately execute a full turn on the forehand using your left leg.

6 After a 360-degree turn, begin forward movement again and ride back out to your initial large circle.

7 Repeat the pattern in the opposite direction.

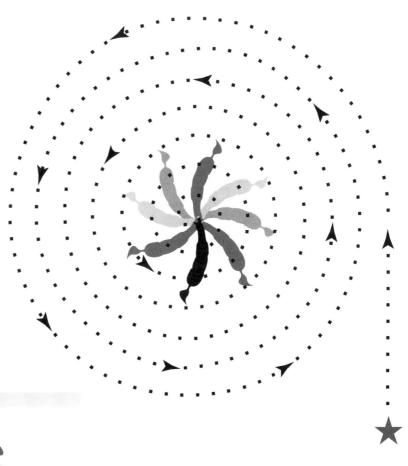

KEY

working walk
· · · · · · · · · ·

turn on forehand

84. Lope Leg-yield

LEVEL: **INTERMEDIATE**

BENEFITS

When a horse lopes with insufficient flexion in his stifle joint, he travels with his inside hind leg carried off to the side of his body rather than swinging it well forward under his trunk. This creates rigidity in his lower back, which hinders the rider from being able to collect him and shift his movement to being balanced on the hind legs.

Exercises like this one help align the inside hind leg under the body in addition to activating the stifle joint. The horse is then balanced properly to move with suppleness in the lope. It assists horses who do not flex their stifles well and can greatly improve balance.

Helpful Hints

★ This is not an exaggerated sideways movement, but more like drifting over.

★ Your horse should maintain forward energy as well as sideways.

★ Do not rush! If your horse tenses, make a circle at any point to soften him.

1 Begin tracking left in a working lope at **B**.

2 At **C**, turn left onto the centerline and proceed straight ahead for a few strides.

3 Leg-yield gradually to the rail at **K**.

4 Continue around the arena and repeat again from **C**.

5 Practice on the right lead as well.

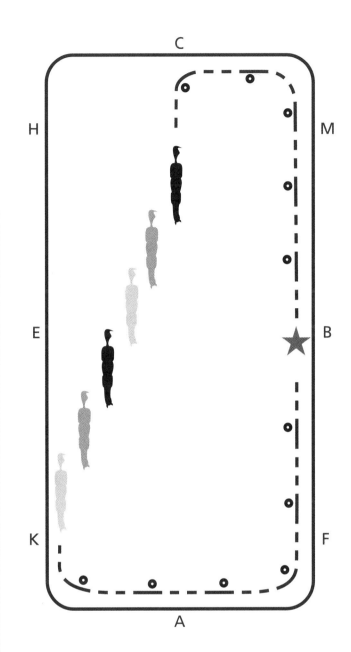

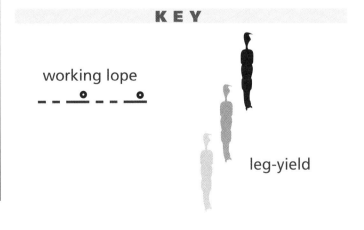

KEY

working lope

leg-yield

85. Elevating Gaits

LEVEL: **INTERMEDIATE**

BENEFITS

This fun and challenging pattern strengthens and stretches the horse's lower lumbar region, those muscles in his loins required to tuck his pelvis. It also increases flexion and strength of his quadriceps, which leads to more stability in stifle and hock joints. When we work on building strength, we are always working equally on increasing suppleness, too. A balanced athlete needs both brawn and elasticity.

Exercises that require the horse to change his stride length and height always improve a horse's body mechanics and rideability. They create a horse that is highly maneuverable and can rapidly but smoothly either collect or extend his gaits, or stop and spin, or anything else you ask. And he is able to do all this without flinging his head up for balance or tilting over sideways like a motorcycle.

Helpful Hints

★ Do not look down at the poles while riding over them!

★ If your horse is hitting the poles with his feet, you need to space them either closer together or farther apart to accommodate his stride.

★ As always, be sure to ride over the center of each pole, not over the outer edges.

1 Set up four poles positioned for your horse's walk stride (approximately 2 feet, 6 inches to 3 feet apart). Also set up four poles positioned for his jog stride (approximately 3 feet, 6 inches to 4 feet apart).

2 Begin at **A** in a medium walk.

3 Cross over the walk poles maintaining good contact. After crossing the last pole, proceed several strides.

4 Transition to a working jog, ride a good bend to the right, and cross over the jog poles.

5 Transition back down to a walk and repeat.

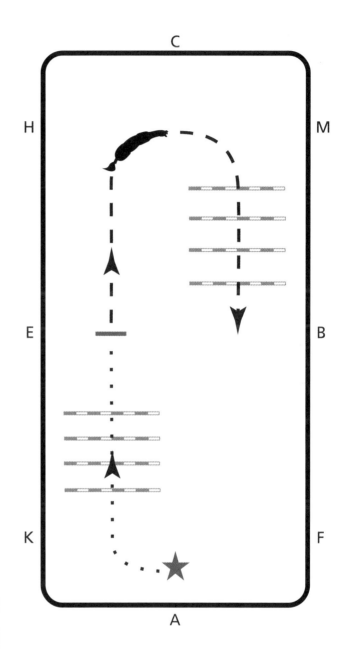

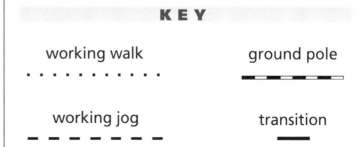

86. Baby Counter-lope

LEVEL: INTERMEDIATE

BENEFITS

Introduce counter-lope with a simple and easily managed exercise so your horse will learn it quickly and without tension. The pattern shown here is the cornerstone for further counter-lope work. If you are unclear how well your horse does or doesn't balance in the counter-lope, this is a great place to start.

Helpful Hints

★ At X, be sure to maintain a left bend as you turn right.

★ Keep your left leg against your horse at the cinch to maintain the left bend.

★ Make sure you do not drift sideways toward M like a leg-yield. Instead, keep a clear line of travel from X to M.

1 Begin at **H** in a working lope, left lead.

2 At **A**, turn down the centerline, maintaining the same tempo.

3 At **X**, turn right on the short diagonal line to **M**. Maintain the left lead on this turn. This creates a minor counter-lope.

4 At **M**, carry on in the left lead.

5 Repeat the pattern in the opposite direction.

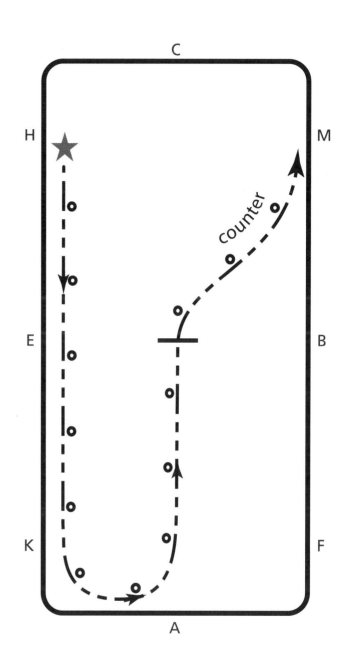

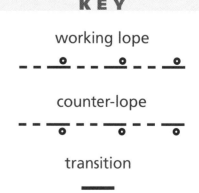

KEY

working lope

counter-lope

transition

87. Counter–True Transitions

LEVEL: **ADVANCED**

BENEFITS

Every rider should master this exercise before tackling flying changes or riding complicated patterns that thread together a lot of collected and counter-lope. This pattern fine-tunes your lope aids and your horse's responsiveness, and progressively loads the hindquarters. Its result is a horse that feels like a hovercraft underneath you.

Helpful Hints

★ Confirm the other counter-lope exercises (numbers 63, 64, and 70) before tackling this one.

★ You will have succeeded when you can reliably and consistently achieve whichever lead you cue.

★ Remember when cueing for each lead that your horse should remain straight in his body, rather than swinging either front or back end sideways. This is why it is most useful to do the exercise along a fence or rail. Once perfect straightness is achieved, begin to expect that your horse will also pick up each lead smoothly while remaining round and on the bit.

★ Remember that each lead is accompanied by your horse's spine being flexed slightly in the direction of his leading leg.

1 Track left at **K** in a collected lope.

2 Continue through the short end in left lead lope.

3 Before **F**, transition to a walk.

4 At **F**, depart in a collected lope, right lead, maintaining a working tempo and right bend.

5 Before **M**, transition to walk.

6 Depart in a collected lope, left lead, and continue through the short end.

7 Keep repeating the pattern.

8 To vary, occasionally transition downward to a jog instead of walk.

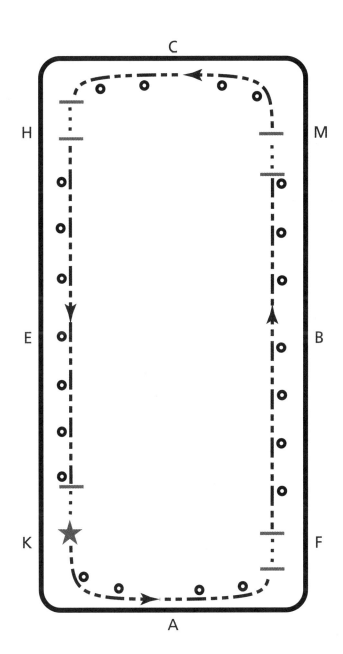

KEY

collected lope

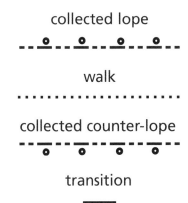

walk

collected counter-lope

transition

88. Double Diagonal

LEVEL: **ADVANCED**

BENEFITS

If your horse's lope suffers from lack of impulsion, roundness, or uphill balance, this exercise will be a challenge — but a good challenge because it will lead to a more balanced lope where your horse is squarely under your seat instead of rushing out the front or bulging to one side. This exercise can brighten up a horse's lope, meaning that it can create more clearly defined steps and a slower cadence from lopes that were otherwise not very lovely to begin with.

This pattern really tests your horse's straightness and responsiveness. It helps to use an arena with a fence or wall around the perimeter to give your horse a visual boundary and help him shift weight into his hindquarters while turning, rather than rushing with choppy strides through the corner. In the absence of a fence, though, you can set up corners for yourself with ground poles, cones, or even a dusting of flour on the sand.

Helpful Hints

★ Your figure should look like a paper clip.

★ If your horse's lope is too quick, he will struggle with this pattern. In this case, tackle it first in the jog.

★ Keep your outside leg *behind* your inside leg. It should remain slightly farther back in order to guide the horse's outside hind leg — which is the propulsive leg and driving force — straight under the horse's body, to act as a guardrail preventing the haunches from swinging outward.

1 Begin at **K** in a working lope, left lead.

2 At **F**, turn as if to cross the diagonal, but aim to arrive at the rail just left of **C**.

3 Turn left at the corner and return across the diagonal at **H**, arriving at the rail to the left of **A**.

4 Maintain a left lead lope for the entire figure.

5 Repeat the pattern in the opposite direction on the right lead.

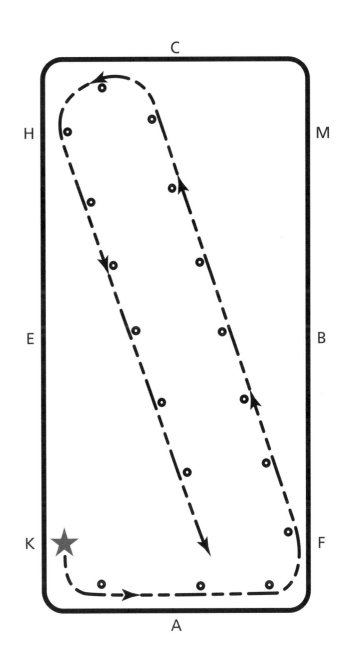

KEY

working lope

- - ○ - - ○ - -

89. Reiner Dressage Circle

LEVEL: **ADVANCED**

BENEFITS

Found in current Western Dressage competition tests, this pattern develops adjustment in the lope. One of the frequent pitfalls of developing collection is that horses get stuck in their movement and begin traveling as though their brakes are always on. This eventually produces stilted or choppy gaits that are slow but without expression or movement through the horse's back. Instead, good collection should grow out of forward energy and vice versa. Collection is always improved by refreshing the horse's energy with small forward surges, such as the ones in this exercise.

Helpful Hints

★ Geometry is critical here. Maintaining bend on the 20-meter circle will help your horse stay round over his topline and therefore lengthen stride better, so do not allow your geometry to get sloppy.

★ Remember to change *your* body when asking your horse to change lope strides. A lengthened lope stride needs a larger, looser movement from your hips, while the collected strides require you to control your hips and make small movements.

1 At **A**, develop working lope, right lead.

2 Proceed to **E** and ride a 20-meter circle.

3 On the 20-meter circle, lengthen the lope steps, aiming to cover as much ground as possible each stride.

4 Then immediately ride a 10-meter circle at **E** in a highly collected lope.

5 Repeat this pattern until your lengthened and collected lopes are clearly differentiated and the changes between each are smooth and prompt.

6 Repeat the pattern on the left lead.

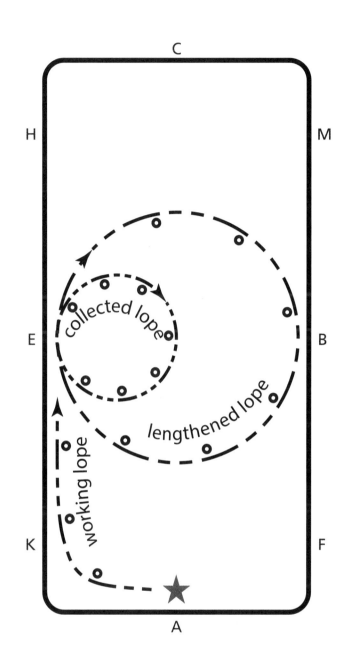

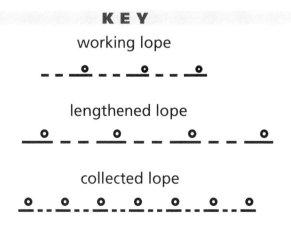

KEY

working lope

lengthened lope

collected lope

90. Flying Changes

LEVEL: **ADVANCED**

BENEFITS

This exercise uses initial transitions to counter-lope to ensure the horse is moving straight through his body without leaning in either direction and without swinging his haunches inward. These transitions help align his haunches under his body, allowing for the flying changes to follow smoothly. See exercise 87: Counter–True Transitions to prepare for flying changes.

Helpful Hints

★ This exercise sets your horse up for the flying change by making him very responsive and engaging him with downward transitions.

★ If he resists making a flying change to the counter-lope, try coming off the rail a bit. Some horses feel like they don't have enough room.

★ Keep your contact and look up.

★ Remember that a flying change is from one collected lope to another, not to a faster tempo.

1 From **A**, proceed in a collected lope, left lead.

2 After **F**, transition to a walk.

3 Immediately depart in a counter-lope.

4 At **M**, transition back to a walk.

5 Immediately resume the left lead.

6 At **E**, set your horse up as if you are going to walk, but then cue for the counter-lope and ride a flying change.

7 Repeat the pattern in the opposite direction.

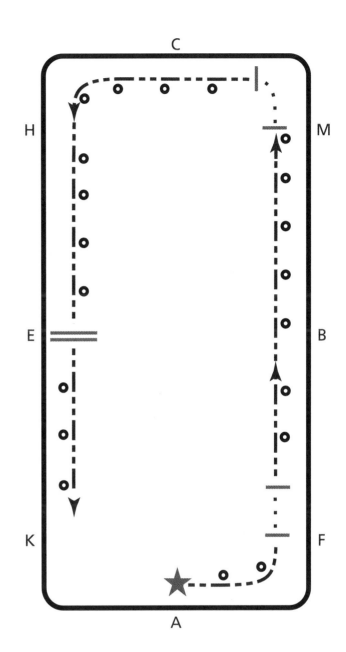

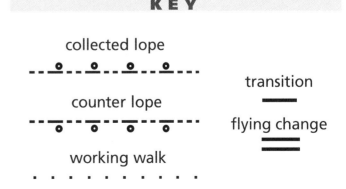

KEY

collected lope

counter lope

working walk

transition

flying change

CHAPTER 7

GROUND WORK

FOR A LONG TIME in the Western tradition, ground work has served as a way not only to introduce new concepts to your horse, such as moving away from and softening to pressure, but also to refine and advance existing skills. Many times, working with your horse on the ground allows you to make progress faster. It eliminates the resistance, confusion, and balance issues that can arise with a rider on his back. This enables him to learn complicated material such as lateral movements and piaffe, for instance, more easily and willingly. It almost goes without saying that this in turn creates a more harmonious partnership between horse and rider, one built on cooperation, trust, and confidence. This directly translates to more success under saddle.

Ground work also serves as a crucial tool for gymnastic development. Especially for the collection, straightness, and suppleness required for dressage, ground work enables you to accomplish things that you might struggle with in the saddle. A crooked or stiff horse, for example, can usually be fixed much more quickly from the ground. He can learn to recruit the correct muscles and joints without interference from a rider. After going through unmounted exercise targeting his specific issues, he is able to produce better movement while carrying a rider.

For the rider's benefit, ground work provides valuable feedback for how the horse is moving and using his body. Some of these nuances are easily missed through relying on feel alone while mounted. While executing exercises on the ground, though, a rider is able to read clearly how her horse responds. For example, she might notice that he braces at the base of his neck when asked for certain maneuvers.

Or he might be more one-sided than she realized. Unmounted, a rider can thoroughly check the horse's alignment during exercises: how quickly his feet move, his responsiveness on each side of his body, his spinal and poll flexion, and so on.

Unfortunately, many riders are already crunched for time and choose to eliminate ground work in favor of riding. It might seem less fun or less important than riding, but the presence of ground work in your regular routine influences whether or not your riding evolves and advances. It might seem tempting to cut it out. But by overlooking its importance, you just might find yourself stuck in a rut with your horse, or at least in your dressage progression.

For horses that have been in training for a while, incorporate ground exercises two days a week into your riding routine. With new or young horses, include 5 to 10 minutes of ground work every day. You can choose one to five favorite exercises with each horse, depending on his individual needs, and rotate through them. When he seems to be performing them with absolute ease, move on to other exercises, so that you are never repeating things robotically.

By focusing on just a few exercises, rather than a vast repertoire, you are much more likely to stick with them and be consistent. Otherwise, with a daunting selection of exercises to choose from, you could become overwhelmed and eschew ground work in preference for something simpler: riding. Find a few ground exercises that target your horse's particular areas of growth and commit one or two days per week to them either as a complement to or replacement for riding those days.

91. Changing Strides In-hand

LEVEL: **BEGINNER**

BENEFITS

Studies show that at rest only 15 percent of a horse's blood flows to his skeletal muscles, the ones responsible for moving his limbs and creating movement. During exercise, that percentage shifts to roughly 85 percent as blood moves from organs and metabolic functions and postural muscles out to these larger muscles. This is what nourishes and powers them, but it takes several minutes of warming the body for this shift in circulation to occur.

Before beginning an active working session, every horse needs to loosen up, a phase during which the emphasis on slow and gentle movements increases circulation of blood, water, and joint fluids (see page 14). This exercise helps take the horse's joints through a full range of motion and releases the locking mechanisms around joints that allow the horse to sleep standing up. From a behavioral standpoint, it also helps him moderate different energy and emotional levels while remaining tuned in to the handler.

Helpful Hints

★ Keep the same tension on your rope as you would have with the reins if you were riding, keeping a soft feel of the horse's head.

★ Make clear changes with your body language to influence your horse.

1 Outfit your horse with a halter and 12-foot lead rope. Walking beside your horse, begin in a 20-meter circle.

2 Walk with short, slow steps, asking your horse to do the same for the first half of the circle.

3 Walk with long, brisk steps and ask your horse to mirror you for the second half of the circle.

4 When you are successful changing walks on the circle, practice the same thing around the track.

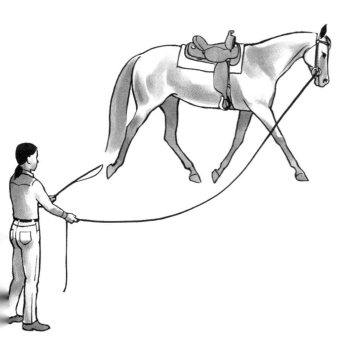

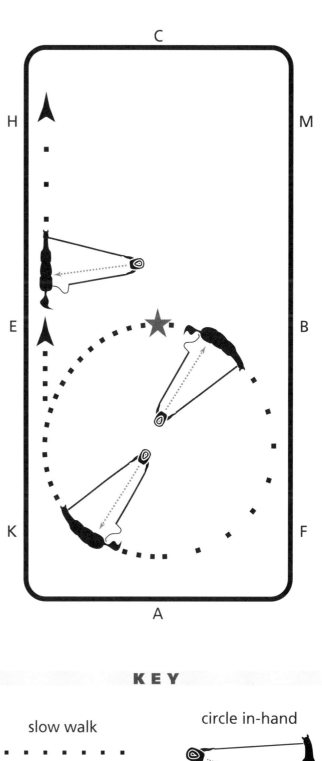

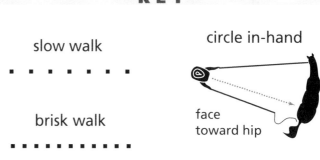

KEY

slow walk

· · · · · · · ·

brisk walk

• • • • • • • • • •

circle in-hand

face toward hip

92. Ground Work Triangle

LEVEL: **BEGINNER**

BENEFITS

In terms of developing better balance and therefore improved movement in our equine athletes, symmetry is a constant priority. Patterns that require a horse to smoothly bend his body from one direction to the other promote evenness in his muscular and skeletal systems. Changing bends while maintaining a slow, steady tempo equalizes how he uses each side of his structure, lessening the dominance on his naturally crooked side.

Small bends done in a quiet tempo (walk only or slow jog with good footing) stretch the horse's long back muscles that span from head to tail, specifically those on the *outside* of the bend. Small bends also require the horse to flex his inside hip and stifle joints in conjunction with flexed obliques and abdominals. The flexed position of these joints requires stabilizing from the adjacent muscle groups and ligaments. This stabilized flexion develops in part from improved strength but also suppleness, which increases from exercises like this one.

Alternating bends from left to right can release tension on the stronger and more dominant side while toning the weaker side. Over time, this alternating muscle recruitment can correct soft-tissue imbalances.

Helpful Hints

★ If you are getting tangled up in your rope, practice the exercise first with a shorter rope and no whip. Once you have become more adept at changing the rope to your new hand when alternating directions, you can carry a whip to help create bend through your horse's rib cage.

★ If the horse leans in or makes "motorcycle turns" rather than bending around each cone, use a stiffer whip such as a bamboo cane to nudge his inside shoulder away from you.

1 Set a cone at each point of a triangle as shown.

2 Outfit your horse with a longe cavesson (or rope halter) and 15- to 20-foot line.

3 Position yourself in the middle of the triangle, and ask your horse to walk a small circle to the right around the top cone on your triangle (cone 1 in diagram).

4 Pass your rope to your left hand and direct the horse to pass in front of you, heading in the direction of cone 2.

5 Circle cone 2 to the left.

6 Pass the horse in front of you again, heading toward cone 3.

7 Circle cone 3 to the right.

8 Continue working your way around the points of the triangle like this. Feel free to mix things up by circling each cone just once or sometimes repeatedly, to keep the horse on his toes and responsive.

9 Start this exercise at the walk and move on to jog and lope as your horse seems ready.

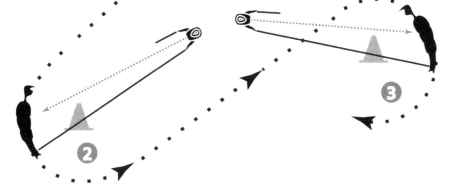

93. Lateral Flexion

LEVEL: **BEGINNER**

BENEFITS

This stretch can prevent your horse from becoming tight in his poll and developing temporomandibular joint disorder (TMJ). When a horse is difficult to bend in one direction when ridden, this exercise almost always remedies the problem. When this exercise is done properly, your horse turns his head from side to side by staying loose in his poll and allowing his head to be independent of his neck. His neck should remain straight and relaxed.

Helpful Hint

★ Take your time. If your horse is stiff, blocked, or guarded, he may resist at first. Don't fight him, but keep gently asking.

1 With your horse bridled, stand facing him.

2 Cradle his head between your hands, placing one lightly on his jaw (not neck) and the other on his nose.

3 Ask him to turn just his head (not his neck) to the left. Ask him to swivel his head, keeping his ears level with the ground.

4 Practice turning his head in the opposite direction, too. One side is often looser than the other.

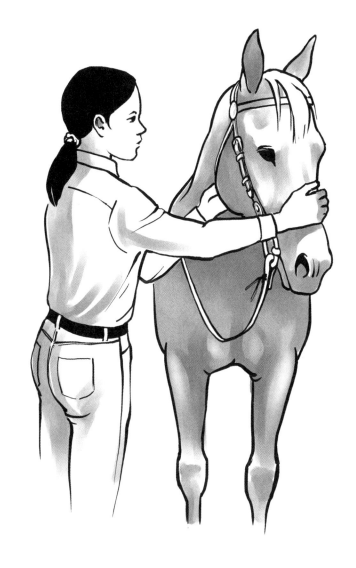

93. Lateral Flexion

94. Cloverleaf

LEVEL: **BEGINNER**

BENEFITS

When helping a horse gain strength, we must focus above all on the recruitment of good postural muscles — the underlying structures that support joints and connect soft tissues. Strength and suppleness in these muscles enables a horse to carry himself well and move with efficiency and lightness. Many training programs focus too much on developing the horse's large gymnastic muscles, which create movement rather than support and carry the horse.

If we strengthen those muscles without equally addressing the underlying muscles supporting the skeleton, the horse will still struggle to carry himself in a good posture. Furthermore, any bracing patterns or restrictions in his movement will continue.

To target the strength and suppleness of postural muscles and to create correct memories in them, utilize slow-paced calisthenics such as this exercise, which asks the horse to keep adjusting his posture. Doing this without a rider allows him to use his body without restriction in these underlying supporting structures. This is when real gains can happen and he is on his way to having more expression and freedom in his movement.

This pattern helps improve your horse's balance by asking him to keep shifting it as you move around each leaf of the cloverleaf. The consistent bending will help create looseness. This pattern also helps relax a horse and develop steady rhythm.

Helpful Hints

★ If your horse rushes through the pattern, add in several walk transitions to gain his attention and keep him responsive to your aids.

★ Be sure your horse is flexing his body in the direction of each turn; you want him turning inward toward each cone as though he were looking at it as he travels past. If needed, use a longe whip to nudge him in the rib cage to develop this flexion.

1 Place a cone at each corner of a 20-meter square and one in the middle of the square. Outfit your horse with a rope halter or longe cavesson and a 20- to 30-foot rope or longe line.

2 Standing near the cone in the middle of the square, ask your horse to longe to the right around the outside of the cones.

3 Back away from the center cone and ask your horse to make an oval that travels around the right top corner cone (1) and the center cone. This is the first "leaf" of your pattern.

4 Shift your position so that you guide your horse to continue around the circle and then make a second oval (2) using the center cone and the bottom right cone.

5 Continue traveling around the pattern this way so that you are making an oval around each cone.

6 Repeat the pattern several times in both directions. When he is comfortable at a walk, try it at a jog.

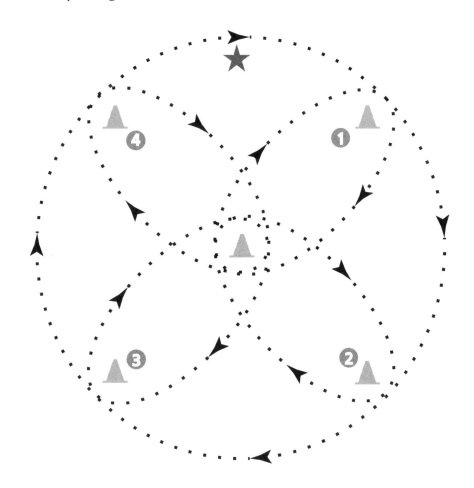

95. Yielding In-hand

LEVEL: **BEGINNER**

BENEFITS

Schooling this movement in-hand allows the horse to take deliberate and precise sideways steps, ensuring that he develops the muscles required for adduction and abduction around his shoulder girdle and chest floor. These are critical muscles for the horse when carrying himself off the forehand and also for more difficult lateral moves such as half-pass. Practicing in-hand also gives you a chance to see whether he executes the same degree of hind-leg crossover in both directions.

Helpful Hints

★ You are *not* looking for a sidepass when you ask your horse to yield. You want each of his steps to cover an *equal* amount of distance forward as well as sideways.

★ Observe whether one direction is easier for your horse than the other — does he yield better and cross his legs more on one side? Also notice if, when you ask him to yield, he lifts his head or braces up. If so, send him back around your small circle to allow the forward motion to soften him, then go back to yielding.

★ Take the time to practice this for just a few moments daily. Most people prefer to practice this exercise as a warm-up, but it is just as effective at the end of your session.

1 Ask your horse to longe around you using a 12-foot rope at the walk.

2 Step closer to him, directing energy at his inside shoulder.

3 Ask him to yield away from you while maintaining the walk.

4 When you get to the rail, make a half-circle, asking your horse to bend his spine away from you.

5 Then step toward him and yield him sideways again.

6 Keep repeating this pattern in both directions. A good guideline is to practice for 3 to 5 minutes before riding.

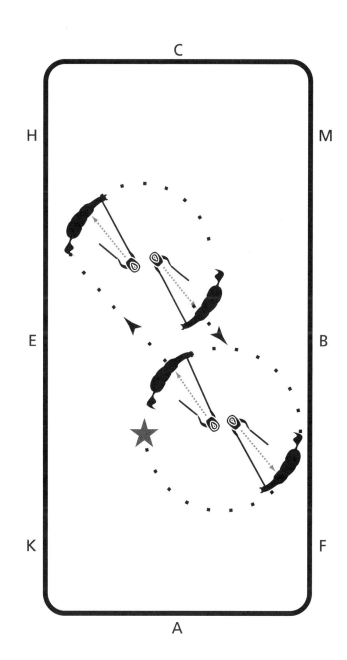

KEY

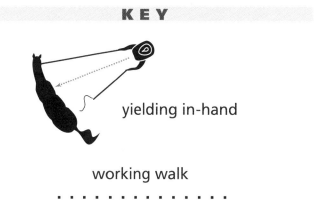

yielding in-hand

working walk
· · · · · · · · · · · · ·

96. Shoulder-in from the Ground

LEVEL: **BEGINNER**

BENEFITS

Without the additional balance constraints of carrying a rider, the horse often offers better engagement
for shoulder-in when schooled from the ground. This
should translate to lowering his inside hip as desired,
which then properly flexes his stifle and hock. The
hamstring muscle group is then recruited properly,
giving stability and tone to all of the hindquarter
joints involved with collection. When a rider's weight
and potentially asymmetrical habits are involved, the
results of shoulder-in are not as consistently reliable.

Helpful Hints

★ Body language and position are
critical. Stand about an arm's
length away to leave space for
your horse's shoulders to step
toward you.

★ In the shoulder-in you will be
working backward, drawing your
horse toward you.

★ The consistent speed of your own
steps determines your success.

1 With your right hand holding the line of your horse's cavesson or rope halter about 3 feet from his chin or nose, face slightly back toward his right hip. With your left hand, point a dressage whip toward his right hock.

2 Ask your horse to walk a small circle around you, close enough for you to touch him with your whip.

3 Using appropriate tension on your line, and laying your whip across his right flank or gaskin, ask his right hind to step deeply under his body by touching it gently. Keep asking him to move around in a complete circle.

4 After the circle, walk a straight line down the rail. Draw your horse's shoulders toward you, keeping his hind legs on the track. Continue like this for several strides.

5 Repeat the exercise in the opposite direction.

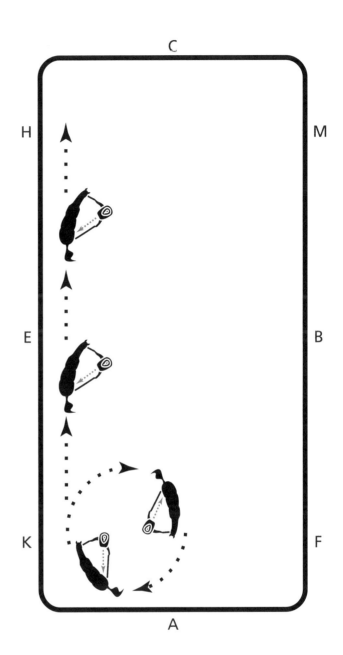

KEY

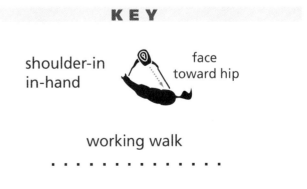

shoulder-in in-hand

face toward hip

working walk
. . . .

97. Varying Circles In-hand

LEVEL: INTERMEDIATE

BENEFITS

This is an in-hand version of a time-tested favorite dressage exercise that calls for varying circle sizes by spiraling in and out. This is an exceptional way to introduce greater engagement to lower-level dressage horses. Further, this dynamic way of longeing the horse prevents him from becoming lazy in his body by going repetitively around the same circle at the same pace. It adds value to the exercise — think of it as working smarter, not harder.

Helpful Hints

★ In part, the quality of your arena footing will determine the success of this exercise. If your footing is hard or slick, do not bring your horse into such a small circle.

★ Ensure that your horse bends his spine more as the circle gets smaller. Use varying tension on your line to achieve this. When necessary — if your horse braces against your line and pulls against your tension — direct your whip toward his hind end and ask him to step underneath his midline with his inside hind leg, which will create bend in his spine.

1 Begin by longeing your horse with a 30-foot rope on a 60-foot circle.

2 After five circles, shorten your rope by 5 feet so that your horse is on a 50-foot circle.

3 Make five circles, then shorten your rope another 5 feet.

4 Continue doing this, eventually having your horse make a 10-meter circle around you.

5 Begin enlarging your circle 5 feet at a time. Gradually, push your horse to the end of your 30-foot rope.

6 Execute in both directions at all three gaits.

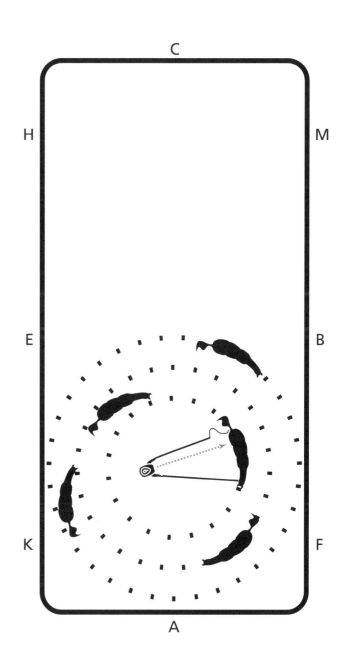

KEY

working walk

circle in-hand

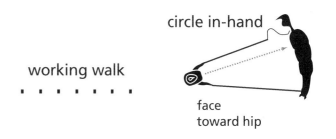

face
toward hip

98. Balance Circles In-hand

LEVEL: INTERMEDIATE

BENEFITS

This ground work exercise shows the horse how to make small adjustments in his body in order to keep himself organized. It also keeps the hind legs working equally and well. By migrating your circles as called for in this pattern, you ask the horse to realign himself in a straight balance before again adopting a bending position. These adjustments, free of a rider's weight, allow him to become more supple.

Helpful Hints

★ Each time you resume circling, ask your horse to flex his spine inward.

★ When you leave the circles, be sure your horse does not speed up. You may need to begin with very short distances.

★ Maintain light tension on your rope, the same as if you were asking for connection with the reins.

1 Jog your horse around you on the end of a 12- or 15-foot rope.

2 Once you develop a good bend and rhythm with your horse, leave the circle and jog alongside your horse for several strides. (Be sure to keep the same rhythm from your circle.)

3 Make another circle, followed by another straight line for several strides.

4 Alternate more circles with straight lines, keeping a steady speed and light tension on the rope.

5 Repeat the exercise in the opposite direction.

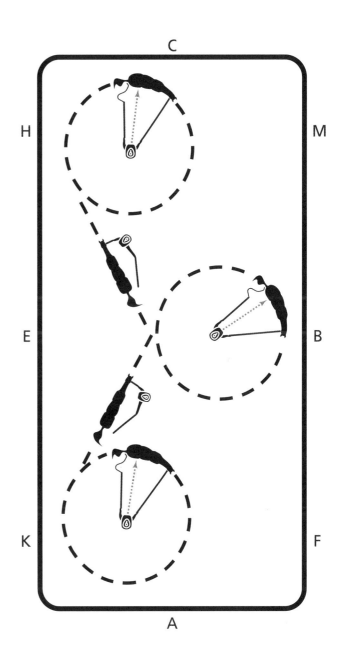

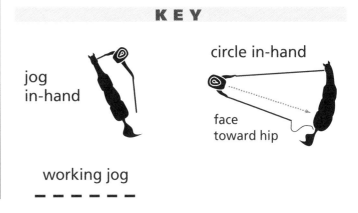

KEY

jog in-hand

working jog

- - - - - -

circle in-hand

face toward hip

99. Leg-yield In-hand

LEVEL: **INTERMEDIATE**

BENEFITS

This foundational exercise shows your horse how to maintain fluidity in lateral movements while also keeping a steady and active amount of energy. Here, an arena fence serves as an assistance aid, allowing the handler to be softer with her cues. The horse learns to balance himself with the visual help of the fence and also learns how to align his body in the correct angle.

Helpful Hints

★ Keep the angle at 45 degrees, no greater!

★ Most horses will try to swing their haunches too far in and subsequently get blocked. At first, you may need to halt your horse after every one or two steps to prevent this.

★ Whenever your horse gets disorganized, halt immediately and reposition him before restarting.

★ Be sure to remain one arm's length away from your horse to direct him, rather than getting "sucked" into his shoulder. If you end up standing too close, you cannot communicate well.

1 Begin standing on your horse's left side at his shoulder. Hold his reins together under his chin in your left hand. With your right hand, reach back with your whip toward his gaskin.

2 Ask him to form a 45-degree angle with his body to the rail with his nose to the fence and his haunches toward the middle of the arena.

3 Ask him to step away from you, maintaining this angle to the fence.

4 Walk down the long side like this. He should cross both front and back legs as he goes.

5 Repeat the exercise in the opposite direction.

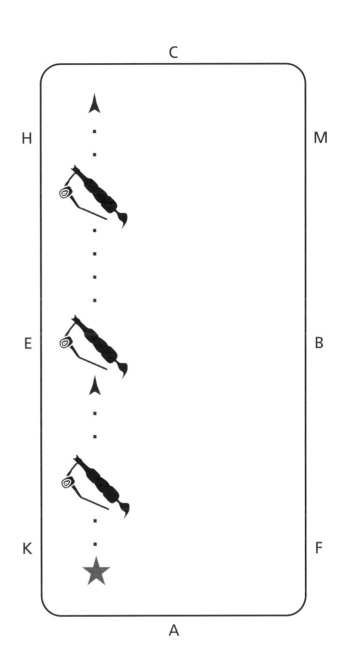

KEY

walk

. . . . . .

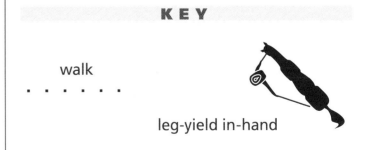

leg-yield in-hand

100. Schaukel In-hand

LEVEL: **ADVANCED**

BENEFITS

In developing any equine athlete, a rider continually needs to think about where the hind legs are. First of all, this demands riding in the correct tempo to build strength. When your horse jogs, watch the motion of his hind legs. Are they swinging forward and landing under his belly or trailing out behind him and landing behind his hip line? If you observe the latter, this indicates poor stifle flexion, and you should increase your tempo during schooling sessions to activate these joints.

The same rule applies to loping, which is why trainers caution riders not to slow the lope tempo before a horse is ready. Without adequate flexion of the joints to draw his hind legs under his belly, it becomes nearly impossible to strengthen his hindquarters.

Once you are riding in the correct tempo for good use of the hind joints, you want to choose exercises that increase strength in the horse's hip flexors, biceps, and quads. Schaukel is an advanced exercise that requires the horse to move from rein-back immediately into a forward gait. As with any gymnastic exercise, use an interval format for this one. Ride it in short doses followed by rest periods of equal duration.

Helpful Hints

★ A good rein-back should look exactly like walking backward with good tempo. The horse should not be too quick, nor should he scrape his feet along the ground.

★ This exercise gets better with regular practice as your horse's response sharpens without becoming abrupt or hollow. With time and multiple repetitions, your horse will lower his haunches as he steps forward in balance.

1 Begin in a quiet halt, standing at your horse's inside shoulder. Use the reins or halter to lower his head and neck to a grounded posture.

2 Back him up four steps. Be sure he backs straight along a fence, without swinging his hips in.

3 Reach back with your whip toward his hind legs and ask him to walk forward four steps.

4 Repeat going backward and forward. Reposition his head and neck if they get high.

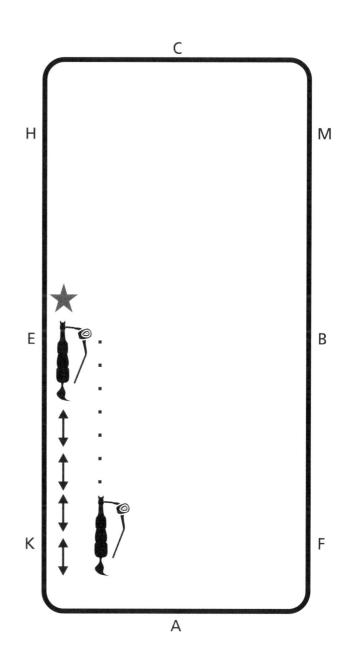

KEY

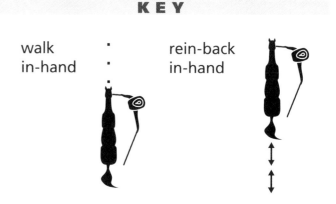

walk in-hand

rein-back in-hand

101. Piaffe Steps

LEVEL: **ADVANCED**

BENEFITS

Without dispute, a horse's ability to flex his sacroiliac joint and lower his haunches entirely determines his success and progress as a performance horse. Flexion and strength here are critical not only for collection, powerful movement, and advanced maneuvers but also for the basic requirement of carrying his rider on a lifted and supple back.

This flexion and suppleness come from a horse's properly using his psoas muscles, those deep interior structures that stabilize his pelvis. This exercise helps a horse achieve the right tone, combined with relaxation that is a cornerstone of good Western Dressage riding.

Helpful Hints

★ Maintain your horse's topline posture as you make the other requests. At any time, you can stop and regain relaxation and roundness.

★ Be sure your horse keeps a consistent response of lifting his leg. If he begins to just barely flex his leg, tap him rhythmically. Let him know you want him to lift it up to the same height each time. Aim for 6 inches off the ground.

★ Each horse responds to being cued at different areas of his body. If you do not get a successful response when cueing as the diagram shows, try asking at a different part of the leg, moving your whip progressively toward his feet. When you find the right spot, praise him immediately and be sure to cue in exactly that same spot the next time.

1 With your horse bridled and your left hand on his noseband, ask him to lower his head and round his neck as you would under saddle. Alternatively, you can hold the reins if your horse accepts this contact quietly.

2 With a long, stiff whip in your right hand, reach back and touch his gaskin area.

3 Ask him to lift that leg up and place it back down.

4 When he does, walk him forward one step.

5 Quickly ask him to lift his leg up again.

6 Walk forward again.

7 Repeat the pattern for a few moments each day until the horse is lifting each back leg as you ask for it. Then practice each day for 30 seconds or more asking him to lift each hind leg as you ask him to walk forward slowly.

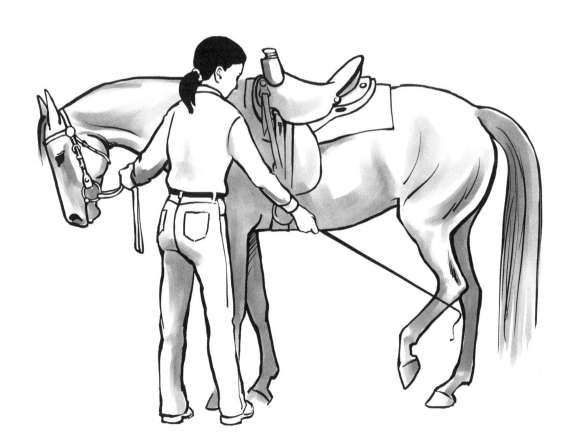

GLOSSARY

Collection. A state in which the horse gathers its body and moves with energy. The strides become shorter and higher as the horse lowers his pelvis toward the ground and increases the flexion of his hind joints. The frame is markedly uphill.

Contact. The horse reaches his head and neck gently out in the direction of the bit in order to create elasticity in the reins with the rider's hands.

Counter-lope. A highly balanced collected lope on the outside lead with proper counter-flexion.

Engagement. The precursor to collection, when the horse shifts his weight back and flexes his joints, allowing him to move forward with power and energy.

Flexion. When the horse yields his jaw and poll, moving his head slightly longitudinally (toward his chest) or laterally (to one side or the other).

Flying lead change. Changing to the opposite lope lead in the space of a single stride without breaking the gait.

Frame. The posture in which the horse carries himself while at work.

Free walk. The horse is given enough rein to completely lower and stretch his head and neck while lengthening his strides and maintaining light contact.

Half-pass. Bending in the direction of travel, the horse moves both sideways and forward with the shoulders slightly leading the haunches.

Haunches-in. The horse moves on four tracks, bent evenly from poll to tail, with his haunches toward the inside of the arena.

Haunches-out. Advanced lateral movement in which the horse moves on four tracks and is bent toward the outside of the arena; the haunches are closest to the rail, while the shoulders travel on an inside track.

Impulsion. The energy and thrust from the engaged hindquarters that drive the horse forward into a collected gait.

Leg-yield. The horse moves both sideways and forward with a very slight counter-flexion.

Massage the rein. Gently working the rein with your fingers as if squeezing water from a sponge.

On the forehand. The horse displaces its body weight to the front legs and pulls itself forward, becoming heavy in the rider's hands.

Pirouette. A 360-degree turn, executed in the walk and the lope, with the horse's hind legs describing a tiny circle as the forehand pivots around.

Rein-back. The horse walks backward in diagonal pairs while remaining round over the topline.

Rhythm. The regularity and sequence of footfalls within a gait. Does not mean tempo or speed.

Schaukel. An advanced exercise that requires the horse to move from rein-back immediately into a forward gait.

Shoulder-in. A lateral movement performed on three tracks with a horse's inside shoulder/foreleg traveling on its own track; the horse is bent toward the middle of the arena.

Sidepass (side step). The horse moves straight sideways with very little forward movement.

Softness. A soft horse responds quickly and willingly to subtle aids; he is aware of his rider at all times.

Suppleness. Flexibility of the joints and muscles; ability to bend easily and comfortably.

Suspension. The moment in the jog or lope when all four hooves are off the ground for an instant. Highly elevated suspension is not sought after in Western Dressage, though gaits are expected to be energetic.

Tempo. Beats per minute of footfalls. Does not refer to the rhythm of footfalls.

Three-loop serpentine. Three half-circles, 20 meters each, connected from one end of the arena to the other. Horse must change bend appropriately for each half-circle.

Tracking left. To travel counter-clockwise.

Tracking right. To travel clockwise.

Turn on the forehand. The horse's front legs remain in place while the hind legs cross markedly as he turns either 180 degrees or 360 degrees.

Turn on the haunches. The horse's haunches remain in place while his front end turns either 180 degrees or 360 degrees.

Working (walk, jog, lope). A pace in which the horse moves energetically but calmly, with a decent length of stride and a rounded topline.

Index

Other Storey Titles You Will Enjoy

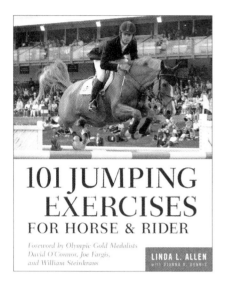

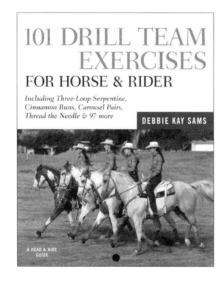

Join the conversation. Share your experience with this book, learn more about Storey Publishing's authors, and read original essays and book excerpts at storey.com. Look for our books wherever quality books are sold or by calling 800-441-5700.